PRESENTED TO

_____

FROM

_____

DATE

_____

Moments of Comfort for the Morning

Moments of comfort for the morning

DAILY REMINDERS
OF GOD'S LOVE AND PROMISES

BETHANYHOUSE
a division of Baker Publishing Group
Minneapolis, Minnesota

Published by Bethany House Publishers
11400 Hampshire Avenue South
Bloomington, Minnesota 55438
www.bethanyhouse.com

Bethany House Publishers is a division of
Baker Publishing Group, Grand Rapids,
Michigan

Previously published under the title *Still
Moments in the Presence of God.*

This edition published 2019

ISBN 978-0-7642-3450-7

Printed in the United States of America

General Editor: Lila Empson Wavering

Cover design by Kathleen Lynch/Black
Kat Design

19   20   21   22   23   24   25   7   6   5   4   3   2   1

GOD'S WAY IS PERFECT. ALL THE LORD'S PROMISES PROVE TRUE. —2 SAMUEL 22:31 NLT

Contents

Introduction

Monetary wealth may be the currency of this world, but it amounts to nothing when compared to God's great and eternal promises. By some counts there are more than 3,500 statements in the Bible that promise benefits for every aspect of our daily lives. We do, indeed, have a good and generous heavenly Father.

The devotions in this volume have been especially written to highlight God's promises. These promises shine light into our lives and give us hope and encouragement. Embrace these promises and experience the power of God in our lives through his words to us.

As you read, we hope you will come to know with certainty that God is eternally invested in all you are and all you do.

MY EYES STAY OPEN THROUGH THE WATCHES
OF THE NIGHT, THAT I MAY MEDITATE ON
YOUR PROMISES. —PSALM 119:148 NIV

There has not failed one

His good

which

through His

word of all

promise,

He promised

ervant Moses.

1 KINGS 8:56 NKJV

Chosen of God

What can we do to win God's approval? Nothing! His approval is already ours in Christ.

A newborn baby doesn't need to jump through any hoops for Mom and Dad to cry tears of joy that a child has been born. God does not reject us because we make mistakes. Parents don't reject a child because she stumbles when she's learning to walk. We serve God not to gain his acceptance but because we already have it.

Our service to God is an offering of gratitude; he has chosen us! We get to be part of the beautiful work he is doing in our world.

EVEN BEFORE HE MADE THE WORLD, GOD LOVED
US AND CHOSE US IN CHRIST TO BE HOLY AND
WITHOUT FAULT IN HIS EYES. —EPHESIANS 1:4 NLT

God, thank you for choosing me, accepting me, and loving me. I choose to serve you because you care for me. Amen.

His Purpose Prevails

MANY ARE THE PLANS IN A PERSON'S
HEART, BUT IT IS THE Lord's PURPOSE THAT
PREVAILS. —PROVERBS 19:21 NIV

We all have hopes and dreams, but often we fail to consider how the flame burning inside us fits into God's bigger plan. Imagine how much more confident we would be if we knew that what we so desperately want for ourselves is what God, too, wants for us.

God's plans are bigger than ours—much bigger. But he has placed in each of us a passion for our particular part in the grand scheme of things.

Your ambitions may be inspired by him. When we give them back to him, we open up a whole new world of possibility.

TAKE DELIGHT IN THE LORD, AND HE
WILL GIVE YOU YOUR HEART'S DESIRES.
—PSALM 37:4 NLT

God, thank you for lighting a fire inside me
and giving me a part to play in your
magnificent plan. Amen.

Always Keeping Watch

FOR HE WILL COMMAND HIS ANGELS
CONCERNING YOU TO GUARD YOU IN ALL
YOUR WAYS. —PSALM 91:11 NRSV

Maybe you've wondered what it would be like to have a bodyguard, to know someone is looking after your safety at all times. After all, it's a dangerous world we live in.

At best, however, a bodyguard's brand of protection is limited. That's why God has chosen to give us divine protection. He has assigned his angels to look after us.

Of course, that doesn't mean bad things will never happen to us. It does mean no one will be able to separate us from God's love or take away our faith or keep us from fulfilling God's plan for our lives. What a wonderful comfort that is.

BLESS THE LORD, O YOU HIS ANGELS,
YOU MIGHTY ONES WHO DO HIS BIDDING.
—PSALM 103:20 NRSV

God, thank you for sending your angels to watch over me. Protect me so that I might serve and love you all my days. Amen.

Angry No More

YOU WILL NOT STAY ANGRY FOREVER, BECAUSE YOU ENJOY BEING KIND. —MICAH 7:18 NCV

Our heavenly Father loves us—delights in us, in fact. We are his family. Like any loving father, God longs for us to take hold of the things that satisfy, the things that bring us peace and joy. And it makes God angry and sad when we willfully take up the things that do us harm.

God isn't vindictive. He doesn't take out his frustrations on his loved ones. But he does hurt when we hurt, and he wants to spare us unnecessary pain and suffering.

All it takes for his anger to subside is to see us turning away from harmful things and walking once again on the right path.

HIS ANGER LASTS ONLY A MOMENT, BUT HIS
FAVOR LASTS A LIFETIME! —PSALM 30:5 NLT

God, thank you for showing your kindness to me.
Thank you for being a loving Father who
always wants the best for me. Amen.

The Spirit's Pledge

BY HIS SPIRIT HE HAS STAMPED US WITH
HIS ETERNAL PLEDGE—A SURE BEGINNING
OF WHAT HE IS DESTINED TO COMPLETE.
—2 CORINTHIANS 1:22 MSG

P apers are signed. Keys are passed across the table.
A valued house is transferred from one person to
another in a real estate closing. The transfer is made possible because both parties affixed their signatures to a
legal contract.

Those signatures signify the new owner's promise to
make payment and the former owner's promise to relin-
quish the property. God's Spirit is like that signature.

When we embrace Jesus as our Lord and Savior, God's
Spirit enters our lives as a guarantee from God that

everything promised to us will one day be ours. But there is one important difference with God. We humans sometimes fail, but God never fails to deliver what he has promised.

THE LOVE OF GOD HAS BEEN POURED OUT IN OUR HEARTS BY THE HOLY SPIRIT WHO WAS GIVEN TO US. —ROMANS 5:5 NKJV

God, thank you for sending your Spirit into my life. I'm glad I can count on you to keep all your promises to me. Amen.

God Will Do It

FAITH IS THE ASSURANCE OF THINGS
HOPED FOR, THE CONVICTION OF THINGS
NOT SEEN. —HEBREWS 11:1 NASB

F lip a light switch, and the light comes on. Sit down in a chair, and the chair provides support. Step on the brake, and the car stops.

Experience has taught us to expect and rely on these things. Our faith teaches us to rely on the promises of God. We don't need to see the end of the story to know that all ends well with God. God has never made a promise to his children that he will not fulfill.

You can rest assured of God's work in your life, his promise of eternal life, and your inclusion in the family of God through your connection with Jesus Christ.

LET US DRAW NEAR TO GOD WITH A SINCERE
HEART AND WITH THE FULL ASSURANCE THAT
FAITH BRINGS. —HEBREWS 10:22 NIV

God, thank you for your assurance that
your promises are true and reliable.
Thank you especially for the assurance
I have in Jesus Christ. Amen.

Given for You

[JESUS CHRIST] IS THE ATONING SACRIFICE FOR OUR SINS, AND NOT ONLY FOR OURS BUT ALSO FOR THE SINS OF THE WHOLE WORLD. —1 JOHN 2:2 NIV

Throughout history good people have been murdered in the name of misplaced zeal, paranoid protection of power, or a demented desire to be in the limelight. Political assassinations and random shootings are rampant in today's world.

Jesus of Nazareth went around healing people and doing good. When he was arrested, he calmly explained that he had no political ambitions or military muscle. He was crucified anyway.

In this case, however, God used the evil actions of misguided people to bring about the greatest triumph of history. Jesus' death served as the sacrifice for our sins. He opened the door to eternal life, and it stands open.

* * * * * * * *

AS FOR OUR TRANSGRESSIONS, YOU WILL PROVIDE ATONEMENT FOR THEM.
—PSALM 65:3 NKJV

* * * * * * * *

God, I praise you for turning tragedy into triumph. Thank you for sending Jesus to atone for my sins. Amen.

Over All the Earth

JESUS CAME TO THEM AND SAID: I HAVE
BEEN GIVEN ALL AUTHORITY IN HEAVEN
AND ON EARTH! —MATTHEW 28:18 CEV

The Bible tells us that Jesus has been given all authority in heaven and earth. What does that mean to us? Simply everything!

It means that no matter what sentence life may hand us—a doctor's daunting diagnosis, an accountant's statement of financial ruin, even our own mind's pronouncement of worthlessness—we can appeal to a higher authority, the court of heaven. And how do we press our case? We remind the court that we carry with us promises backed in full by the great God of creation.

No matter what we face in life, we need not fear. We can take all our concerns to Jesus.

THERE IS NO AUTHORITY EXCEPT FOR GOD,
AND THE AUTHORITIES THAT EXIST ARE
APPOINTED BY GOD. —ROMANS 13:1 NKJV

God, thank you for allowing me to bring my concerns to you. I recognize your authority over every aspect of this life. Amen.

When You Believe

THEN JESUS TOLD HIM, "YOU BELIEVE BECAUSE YOU HAVE SEEN ME. BLESSED ARE THOSE WHO BELIEVE WITHOUT SEEING ME." —JOHN 20:29 NLT

In this world, it's often difficult to know whom we can believe in. Fortunately, there is someone we can reach out to. That person is God. But how do we know he's real?

When we were created, God placed in each of us a spirit. This is what makes us like him and unlike his other creatures. When we surrender ourselves to him, our spirits come to life, and that living spirit inside us bears witness that he is who he says he is. That's all the evidence we need.

We don't have to see with our eyes what we have seen with our hearts.

WHOEVER BELIEVES IN HIM WILL NOT BE
DISAPPOINTED. —ROMANS 10:11 NASB

God, I believe in you. I believe you are
fixing the things that are broken in my life
and in my world. Thank you! Amen.

Buried with Christ

WHEN WE CAME UP OUT OF THE WATER,
WE ENTERED INTO THE NEW COUNTRY OF
GRACE—A NEW LIFE IN A NEW LAND!
—ROMANS 6:3 MSG

In the movie *The Princess Diaries*, a shy awkward teen, Mia Thermopolis, wakes up to discover that she is royalty—heir to the throne of Genovia. One day she's struggling with school bullies and driving lessons; the next she has a bodyguard and chauffeur. Everything changes.

That's something like what happens when we decide to follow Christ. God invites us into a life as his own royal child. Those bullies who would condemn us are gone. We are protected and directed by God's Holy Spirit.

Baptism sends the message that everything has changed. The old is gone. You have a new, royal life in Christ.

WHEN WE ARE RAISED UP OUT OF THE WATER,
IT IS LIKE THE RESURRECTION OF JESUS.

—ROMANS 6:4 MSG

God, I accept and thank you for the new life you have offered me in Jesus. Please be honored in everything I do. Amen.

He Knows His Own

IT IS [GOD] WHO HAS MADE US, AND NOT WE
OURSELVES; WE ARE HIS PEOPLE AND THE
SHEEP OF HIS PASTURE. —PSALM 100:3 NKJV

If you've ever felt left out, excluded, and disrespected, then you are in good company. Jesus himself knows what it's like to be rejected. He was not only ostracized and ridiculed by the popular and the powerful men of his day, but he was also crucified by them. The great heroes of the Bible, Jesus tells us, experienced the same kind of treatment.

But when you choose to become part of God's family, he welcomes you with open arms. You have a place in his heart, a seat at his table, a role in his kingdom.

No one can take your place. You matter. You belong.

GOD MAKES SURE THAT WE ALL EXPERIENCE
WHAT IT MEANS TO BE OUTSIDE SO THAT
HE CAN PERSONALLY OPEN THE DOOR AND
WELCOME US BACK IN. —ROMANS 11:32 MSG

God, thank you for welcoming me into
your family. I'm glad you have given
me a place in your kingdom. Amen.

His Many Gifts

PRAISE THE LORD, MY SOUL, AND FORGET
NOT ALL HIS BENEFITS. —PSALM 103:2 NIV

For two years, a $100,000 yacht remained moored in a marina in the Swedish village of Stromstad. The keys were in plain sight, but the owner was nowhere to be seen. Authorities tracked down every lead to determine who was responsible for the boat. When they finally found the owner—in a different country—he admitted that he thought he had sold the boat. He had totally forgotten that he still owned it.

We can't enjoy what we forget we own.

God invites us to remember what belongs to us as a way of calling us back to the joy that is our birthright as sons and daughters of God.

MAY ALL THE GIFTS AND BENEFITS THAT COME
FROM GOD OUR FATHER, AND THE MASTER,
JESUS CHRIST, BE YOURS. —1 CORINTHIANS 1:3 MSG

God, thank you for the love, forgiveness, and
healing that overflow in the new life
that is mine in Jesus Christ. Amen.

Friendly Lines

YOU HAVE GIVEN HIM BLESSINGS THAT
WILL LAST FOREVER, AND YOU HAVE MADE
HIM GLAD BY BEING SO NEAR TO HIM.
—PSALM 21:6 CEV

While on a reconnaissance mission during the Vietnam War, a young marine was separated from his company. For several hours he wandered through a tangled maze of tropical forest before he finally found his way back to friendly lines.

Finding God is like finding our way back to friendly lines. We can relax because God blesses us with protection from the things that would destroy us and with provision for all our needs.

As we grow, we make an important discovery. Hidden among God's many blessings is the greatest blessing of all—his enduring presence. His love opens the door to a beautiful friendship that will last for all eternity.

* * * * * * *

WHAT MUST I GIVE YOU, LORD, FOR BEING SO GOOD TO ME? —PSALM 116:12 CEV

* * * * * * *

God, thank you for giving me the best blessing of all—your presence in my life both now and throughout eternity. Amen.

Building the Inner You

ENDURANCE PRODUCES CHARACTER, AND
CHARACTER PRODUCES HOPE. —ROMANS 5:4 NRSV

Good personal trainers know just how hard to push. They know we won't grow by staying in our comfort zone. That's why they call on us to increase the weight, do another set, increase the repetitions.

They can see past the process to the results. They know how to connect all that hard work with the great feeling that comes from being trim, fit, and full of energy.

God is a trainer as well, a trainer of our souls, and he knows how hard to push. God looks past the pain and points to his promise of character that will be ours when we have learned to overcome our trials through the grace he provides.

KEEP A FIRM GRASP ON BOTH YOUR CHARACTER
AND YOUR TEACHING. DON'T BE DIVERTED. JUST
KEEP AT IT. —1 TIMOTHY 4:16 MSG

God, thank you for coaching me. Please empower me to get the full benefit of the lessons you are teaching me about character. Amen.

Looking Up

BE CHEERFUL NO MATTER WHAT; PRAY ALL
THE TIME; THANK GOD NO MATTER WHAT
HAPPENS. —1 THESSALONIANS 5:16–17 MSG

W hat's the big deal about being cheerful?" you
ask. "Look around you and all you see is greed
and materialism and immorality. Neighbors killing
neighbors, religious zealots killing just because they
can. What exactly do we have to be cheerful about?"

The world has always been a daunting place. It probably always will be. But God says in his Word that he
has conquered the world. He has promised us joy in the
midst of tragedy, happiness in bitter circumstances,
and victory in the face of defeat. God alone has power
over our lives. When we belong to him, we are subject
to no other. That's something to be cheerful about!

A CHEERFUL HEART FILLS THE DAY
WITH SONG. —PROVERBS 15:15 MSG

God, though I live in the midst of this troubled world, my life is in your hands and yours alone. That makes me smile. Amen.

God's Promise

of Love

MY UNFAILING LOVE FOR YOU WILL
NOT BE SHAKEN
NOR MY COVENANT OF PEACE BE
REMOVED. —ISAIAH 54:10 NIV

The Little Ones

GOD-LOYAL PEOPLE, LIVING HONEST LIVES,
MAKE IT MUCH EASIER FOR THEIR CHILDREN.
—PROVERBS 20:7 MSG

The more we experience God's love, the more we love God in return. Letting ourselves be loved by God heals all kinds of hurts, renews our minds, and transforms our lives. We become different people.

This transformation we experience has a ripple effect. Starting with those closest to us, others are drawn to the new life God has placed inside us.

That's why parents who love God give their children a precious gift. They bring the sunshine of God's presence into the lives of their children. God's love is a promise fulfilled not only in our lives but also in the lives of our children.

HIS MERCY IS ON THOSE WHO FEAR HIM FROM
GENERATION TO GENERATION. —LUKE 1:50 NKJV

God, please let me experience your love in a deeper way so I can love you and others more and more. Amen.

Clean before God

GOD MADE MY LIFE COMPLETE WHEN
I PLACED ALL THE PIECES BEFORE HIM.
WHEN I CLEANED UP MY ACT, HE GAVE ME
A FRESH START. —2 SAMUEL 22:21–22 MSG

During a 1987 yacht race, Ian Kiernan from Australia was looking forward to seeing the beauty of the Sargasso Sea in the North Atlantic Ocean. Instead of beauty, however, he encountered trash and pollution.

Some people would be disgusted, but the trash motivated Kiernan. Returning to Australia, he organized Clean Up Sydney Harbour Day, which mobilized forty thousand volunteers to remove trash and restore the beauty of the area.

When God sees things in us that defile us, he never turns away in disgust. Instead, when we remove the trash in our lives, he restores the beauty of the real person in us. There isn't any life that God can't cleanse if we turn everything over to him.

WASH ME THOROUGHLY FROM MY INIQUITY AND CLEANSE ME FROM MY SIN. —PSALM 51:2 NASB

God, thank you for your promise to cleanse me and make something beautiful of my life. Thank you for loving the real me. Amen.

He Is with You

I FEAR NO EVIL: FOR YOU ARE WITH
ME: YOUR ROD AND YOUR STAFF—
THEY COMFORT ME. —PSALM 23:4 NRSV

For a small child in a healthy family, a mother's comfort is one of the anchors in his life. Scraped knees, bullies on the playground, monsters in the closet, or scary dreams—these things send a little one back to Mom, where he receives the care and reassurance that everything is going to be okay.

As we grow, we learn a different level of comfort—God's comfort. The bullies now are different: serious disease, loss and grief, financial hardship, relational disasters. But God's comfort remains the same.

He cares for us. He tells us the comforting truth. And his promises reassure us that everything will ultimately be okay.

* * * * * * *

PRAISE BE TO THE GOD AND FATHER OF OUR LORD JESUS CHRIST, THE FATHER OF COMPASSION AND THE GOD OF ALL COMFORT. –2 CORINTHIANS 1:3 NIV

* * * * * * *

God, thank you for comforting me in my times of trouble. I'm glad that I am safe with you. Amen.

Sticking with It

WHAT HAPPENS WHEN WE LIVE GOD'S WAY? . . .
WE DEVELOP A WILLINGNESS TO STICK WITH
THINGS. . . . WE FIND OURSELVES INVOLVED IN
LOYAL COMMITMENTS. —GALATIANS 5:22–23 msg

You don't get much sleep if you're walking the floor at night with a crying baby. Changing diapers is hardly a favorite activity. Answering an endless stream of questions from a preschooler can test anyone's patience.

No one ever said parenting is easy. But most parents wouldn't trade it for anything in the world. Love for their children causes them to barely notice the cost.

Likewise, no one ever said the Christian life is easy. But we don't give up. Our love for Jesus shrinks our sacrifices and magnifies our joy. There is just one way to live this life—all in. That's God's commitment to us as well.

ONCE THE COMMITMENT IS CLEAR, YOU DO WHAT
YOU CAN, NOT WHAT YOU CAN'T. THE HEART
REGULATES THE HANDS. —2 CORINTHIANS 8:12 MSG

God, give me, please, the persistence to stick with the moment—by—moment choices that you put before me daily. Amen.

Holding Fast

LET US HOLD FAST THE CONFESSION OF OUR
HOPE WITHOUT WAVERING, FOR HE WHO
PROMISED IS FAITHFUL. —HEBREWS 10:23 NKJV

On a summer day in 2007, an Air National Guard
pilot flew his F-15A fighter plane into the Pacific
Ocean at more than 600 mph. The pilot was killed, and
the 32-million-dollar aircraft destroyed. If the pilot
made a distress call, it wasn't soon enough for a verbal exchange.

Investigators determined the pilot—with tragic
results—ignored his vital instruments, experienced
spatial disorientation, and misjudged where he was
and what direction he was going. When God seems far
away and life seems upside down, hold fast to your
confession of faith. Trust in God and his promises. He
will keep you on track and get you safely home.

TAKE HOLD OF THE ETERNAL LIFE TO WHICH
YOU WERE CALLED WHEN YOU MADE YOUR
GOOD CONFESSION IN THE PRESENCE OF MANY
WITNESSES. —1 TIMOTHY 6:12 NIV

God, keep me focused on you and the clear
promises and instructions you have given me
in your Word, the Bible. Amen.

Standing with Confidence

DO NOT CAST AWAY YOUR CONFIDENCE, WHICH HAS GREAT REWARD. —HEBREWS 10:35 NKJV

Sooner or later you will face bullies in life that are bigger than you are. That's reality. The bullies may come in the form of pain and disease, fractured relationships, financial disaster, or some other challenge.

The strongest people realize their strength has limits. Our ability to cope is finite. But we serve a God who can triumph in us regardless of our circumstances. God hears our prayers and rewards us with the will and the strength to persevere.

Our confidence is not in our own abilities, but rather in the God who has promised to keep us safe in his arms for all of eternity.

IN THE FEAR OF THE LORD THERE IS STRONG CONFIDENCE, AND HIS CHILDREN WILL HAVE REFUGE. —PROVERBS 14:26 NASB

God, thank you that I can put my confidence in you. I know nothing can happen to me that you can't handle. Amen.

Choppy Water

YOUR COURAGE AND UNITY WILL SHOW
THEM WHAT THEY'RE UP AGAINST: DEFEAT
FOR THEM, VICTORY FOR YOU—AND BOTH
BECAUSE OF GOD. —PHILIPPIANS 1:29 MSG

Throughout history, people have become followers of Jesus Christ by observing how people of faith handle conflict. Even today, there are reports of terrorists who turned to Christ because of the courage and love they observed in the Christians they persecuted.

The confidence you have in God, the way you overcome your fears, the way you forgive those who act against you—all of these things speak to your beliefs and values.

In every difficult circumstance, God has promised to stand beside those who trust him. With him by your side, you are already victorious now and in the greater life to come.

* * * * * * * *

OVERWHELMING VICTORY IS OURS THROUGH CHRIST, WHO LOVED US. —ROMANS 8:37 NLT

* * * * * * * *

God, I need you to face the challenges of my life with me. Thank you for giving me the strength I need to overcome adversity. Amen.

Questions! Questions!

I WILL PRAISE THE Lord, WHO COUNSELS
ME; EVEN AT NIGHT MY HEART INSTRUCTS
ME. —PSALM 16:7 NIV

Imagine what it would be like to walk into a classroom
to take an exam, knowing that you are unprepared.
You sit down at your desk with a sinking feeling in your
stomach, realizing you will probably fail the test.

In the course of our lives, most of us encounter
situations where we feel unprepared, over our heads,
in the dark. We don't have to accept failure, however,
if we have a relationship with God. He won't take the
test for us, but he is glad to help us make sense of
things, at least enough to move forward.

All we have to do is ask.

WITH YOUR COUNSEL YOU WILL GUIDE ME.

—PSALM 73:24 NASB

God, thank you for your guidance. Please help me to understand the things you are teaching me as you guide me through life. Amen.

Standing Strong

BE STRONG, AND LET YOUR HEART
TAKE COURAGE, ALL YOU WHO WAIT FOR
THE LORD. —PSALM 31:24 NRSV

Courage is a gift from God. We aren't born with the strength to say no to our fears and to do what is right regardless of the cost. That strength is given to us from above in our time of need.

God knows how fragile we are. Jesus was fully divine and fully human. As a man, he didn't like pain any more than any other human does. But he went to the cross and its excruciating pain voluntarily. His eleven faithful disciples also faced their fears, and they received the strength to overcome.

We wait for God in our time of need, because in him we find strength.

DO NOT BE AFRAID, NOR BE DISMAYED,
FOR THE LORD YOUR GOD IS WITH YOU
WHEREVER YOU GO. —JOSHUA 1:9 NKJV

God, I am weak, but you are strong. Grant me, I pray, the strength to follow you no matter the cost. Thank you. Amen.

Bound Up with God

HE PROVIDED REDEMPTION FOR HIS PEOPLE;
HE ORDAINED HIS COVENANT FOREVER.

—PSALM 111:9 NIV

Our world is broken. Wars, disease, poverty, hatred, hurt, strife—the list of things that need to be fixed is long and depressing. But God isn't deterred by any of these problems. He has initiated a covenant relationship with those who commit their lives to him, and he won't violate it.

No matter how bad things get in the world around us, God has sworn an oath—that's what *covenant* means—never to leave us stranded without hope. He has set in place a beautiful plan to redeem us, and he will see it through to the end.

You can believe his word for a thousand generations!

THE Lord YOUR GOD, HE IS GOD, THE FAITHFUL
GOD WHO KEEPS COVENANT AND MERCY FOR
A THOUSAND GENERATIONS WITH THOSE WHO
LOVE HIM. —DEUTERONOMY 7:9 NKJV

God, I praise you because you keep your word.
Thank you for your work in restoring and
transforming me. Amen.

Good Choices

USE COMMON SENSE AND SOUND JUDGMENT!
ALWAYS KEEP THEM IN MIND. –PROVERBS 3:21 CEV

S top, look, and listen" is excellent advice to take before starting across the street. It's also something to remember as we make important decisions.

Stop to consider how our decision might shape the future. Can we foresee any adverse or unintended consequences? *Look* at the message our choice may send to others. Will our actions negatively affect others or our relationships with them? Most of all, *listen* to what God says. Are there commandments or guidelines in Scripture relevant to the choices in front of us?

God promises to give his wisdom to everyone who asks—everyone. Good choices are only a prayer away.

NOT AS I WILL, BUT AS YOU WILL.

—MATTHEW 26:39 NKJV

God, grant me the ability to stop, look, and listen before making choices that affect my life and the lives of others. Amen.

Deliver Me, Lord!

THE RIGHTEOUS PERSON MAY HAVE MANY
TROUBLES, BUT THE LORD DELIVERS HIM
FROM THEM ALL. —PSALM 34:19 NIV

Trouble comes to all of us, believers and non-believers alike. Burdens weigh on those who faithfully follow the rules and those who willfully transgress them. The difference lies in our attitude toward the challenges that confront us.

Faith in God's compassion and his power to help means that we are never alone when we're dealing with difficulties. We can call on him and know that he listens and answers. When we leave our worries and frustrations in his hands, we can rest easy, confident that he will stir in us patience, acceptance, and strength as he leads us through to the end.

In his way and in his time, God delivers.

YOU SEE, THE LORD KNOWS HOW TO RESCUE GODLY
PEOPLE FROM THEIR TRIALS. —2 PETER 2:9 NLT

God, deliver me from anxiety and despair when trouble comes my way. Let me rely on your strength and power to save me. Amen.

Healing Comfort

I SOUGHT THE LORD, AND HE HEARD ME,
AND DELIVERED ME FROM ALL MY FEARS.
—PSALM 34:4 KJV

We all get the blahs from time to time. But some of us also suffer from despair and with great severity. While those who despair may require the intervention of a physician or counselor, the spiritual health and emotional well-being of both them and those who simply get the blahs now and again are affected.

When we're feeling down, we can bring our sadness to God. We can express our feelings to him, just as we would to a trusted friend.

Although God sees inside our hearts, we benefit from consciously and willingly exploring our deepest feelings with him. Hold nothing back. God cares about how you feel, and he has promised you rest in his strong arms.

IF YOU ARE CHEERFUL, YOU FEEL GOOD; IF YOU ARE SAD, YOU HURT ALL OVER. —PROVERBS 17:22 CEV

God, when my heart is heavy with dullness and despair, draw me close to you, the source of renewal and regeneration. Amen.

The Lord Satisfies

YOU SATISFY THE DESIRES OF ALL YOUR
WORSHIPERS, AND YOU COME TO SAVE THEM
WHEN THEY ASK FOR HELP. —PSALM 145:19 cev

In the drugstore, a two-year-old girl was screaming and thrashing about. She couldn't understand why her mother refused to buy her an adult cosmetic gift set. Was the mother being mean? Not at all.

We don't always know what we really want, but God does. We bring our desires—good and bad—to him, knowing that he satisfies those desires with good things.

As we grow, our desires grow with us. We begin to better understand what things are truly desirable. Our need for trinkets and toys gives way to a desire to bring good into our world and to be a blessing to the ones we love. God delights in satisfying these desires.

DELIGHT YOURSELF ALSO IN THE LORD, AND
HE SHALL GIVE YOU THE DESIRES OF YOUR
HEART. —PSALM 37:4 NKJV

God, please give me a heart that desires the things you desire. Thank you for satisfying my desires with good things. Amen.

God's Promises

f Joy

THOSE THE LORD HAS RESCUED WILL RETURN.
THEY WILL ENTER ZION WITH SINGING;
EVERLASTING JOY WILL CROWN THEIR HEADS.
—ISAIAH 35:10 NIV

Fight-or-Flight

WE KNOW THAT SUFFERING PRODUCES
PERSEVERANCE; PERSEVERANCE, CHARACTER;
AND CHARACTER, HOPE. —ROMANS 5:3–4 NIV

Psychologists call it fight-or-flight. It's the instinct we have in any threatening situation to run away or to stay and fight.

In every spiritual journey, we come across difficult times—times when instinct urges us to give up or run away. What you do when you encounter those moments will determine how successful you are in your spiritual walk. Did you think God would fight every spiritual battle for you? The truth is, he will; he is with you while it's happening.

He knows that when you take part in the struggle, you will also take part in the victory.

God, grant me the willingness, strength, and
tenacity to persevere without complaint or
sluggishness, especially when the end
seems far away. Amen.

My Heart Is Yours

PRESERVE MY LIFE, FOR I AM DEVOTED TO
YOU; SAVE YOUR SERVANT WHO TRUSTS IN
YOU. YOU ARE MY GOD. —PSALM 86:2 NRSV

Genuine devotion is marked by from-the-heart words and actions. If we're devoted to a person, we show our affection in real and practical ways. If we're devoted to a cause, we not only support it by any means we can, but we do our best to attract others.

Devotion to God includes private prayer and personal reflection, but that isn't all. Devotion expresses itself in real-world speech and action, conduct, and relationships. We're prompted to invite our friends to know God better and discover the depth of his love.

We're compelled to live according to his rules, serving as an example to others.

When the heart is devoted to God, it shows.

* * * * * * * *

FEAR THE LORD, AND SERVE HIM IN TRUTH WITH ALL YOUR HEART: FOR CONSIDER WHAT GREAT THINGS HE HAS DONE FOR YOU. —1 SAMUEL 12:24 NKJV

* * * * * * * *

God, let my devotion to you be visible so others may come to know your love and your promises. Amen.

Understanding God's Ways

I AM YOUR SERVANT; GIVE ME DISCERNMENT
THAT I MAY UNDERSTAND YOUR STATUTES.
—PSALM 119:125 NIV

Scripture tells us how God interacted with people in biblical times. Those interactions are historical facts. Spiritual discernment, however, develops as we take what Scripture says about the past and apply it to our present circumstances.

We may not find a clear teaching in the Bible that specifically addresses a situation we're facing right now, and that's where discernment comes in. The more we read and reflect on God's teachings, the sharper our ability becomes to perceive their larger, universal meanings.

Through his Spirit's work in us, we're able to connect what he has said and done in the past to his will and counsel today.

* * * * * * * *

BE SMART AND LEARN WHAT TO DO AND
WHEN TO DO IT. —ECCLESIASTES 8:5 CEV

* * * * * * * *

God, sharpen my ability to discern your good counsel in my present circumstances, and, as you have promised, grant me the wisdom to apply it. Amen.

God's Hand of Love

DO NOT REGARD LIGHTLY THE DISCIPLINE
OF THE LORD . . . FOR THE LORD DISCIPLINES
THOSE WHOM HE LOVES. —HEBREWS 12:5–6 NRSV

No one likes correction! When someone points out a mistake we've made, we often feel embarrassed and even diminished. Yet owning up to mistakes and learning from them are marks of a confident, mature person.

God, desiring our spiritual confidence and maturity, has promised to show us when we make mistakes. Perhaps he'll use our conscience to convict us, or use adverse results to afflict us. The Bible or another person may tell us we have done wrong, or a devastating consequence may give us pause to consider our words and actions.

Spiritual correction isn't pleasant, but it is God's hand of love inviting us back to him.

IF YOU REJECT DISCIPLINE, YOU ONLY HARM YOUR-
SELF; BUT IF YOU LISTEN TO CORRECTION, YOU
GROW IN UNDERSTANDING. — PROVERBS 15:32 NLT

God, never let me ignore your discipline, but let me take it seriously, learn from it, and make the needed changes in my life. Amen.

God Is Faithful

WHAT IF SOME DID NOT BELIEVE? WILL
THEIR UNBELIEF MAKE THE FAITHFULNESS
OF GOD WITHOUT EFFECT? CERTAINLY NOT!
—ROMANS 3:3–4 NKJV

God is faithful. He never makes a promise he cannot or will not keep. His mood and his attitude toward us never vary with the passage of time. We all know this isn't true in our human relationships!

Many among us have been deeply hurt by the unfaithfulness of someone close to us. Sometimes we have been proven unfaithful because our feelings, perception, or circumstances shifted. But when we turn to God, we need never doubt his loyalty. Whether we come with a heart broken by betrayal, or a repentant soul burdened by our own unfaithfulness, he is there.

God is God, separate from our failings and weaknesses. He is 100 percent faithful.

WHEN DOUBTS FILLED MY MIND, YOUR COMFORT GAVE ME RENEWED HOPE AND CHEER. —PSALM 94:19 NLT

God, forgive me for the times I have been unfaithful to you and to others, as I forgive those who have been unfaithful to me. Amen.

Investing in Dreams

SUSTAIN ME, MY GOD, ACCORDING TO YOUR
PROMISE, AND I WILL LIVE; DO NOT LET MY
HOPES BE DASHED. —PSALM 119:116 NIV

Dreaming is a wonderful thing. It's pleasant
to sit back and visualize our hearts' desires,
which could be relaxing on a tranquil beach, welcoming a new baby, or landing a plum promotion. In our
dreams, anything is possible.

God doesn't promise to make all our dreams come
true, but he does promise that he has good plans
for us. Through the contours and crossroads of our
dreams, he often leads us to even greater possibilities.
In the vistas and voyages of our imagination, he can
help us discover our true destiny.

Sit back and spend time exploring your dreams.
When God inspires them, it's time well invested.

THERE SHALL BE SHOWERS OF BLESSING.

—EZEKIEL 34:26 KJV

God, it's a pleasure to share my dreams with you, because I know that your desire for me is spiritual joy and eternal salvation. Amen.

Lifted Up

DON'T GIVE UP, BECAUSE YOU WILL GET
A REWARD FOR YOUR GOOD WORK.
—2 CHRONICLES 15:7 NCV

When things are going downhill," someone once quipped, "don't go down with them!" It's hard to stop the nosedive, however, when discouragement flags our spirit and sinks our hopes.

The power of God and his promises come together to lift our spirit. With renewal that begins in the heart, God invites us to rest in his loving embrace. In him, we can take our eyes off whatever is going downhill and instead look upward to the plans and possibilities he puts in front of us.

Be encouraged. Things may be headed in the wrong direction, but God has only one direction for you, and that's up.

· · · · · · · ·

THE SCRIPTURES GIVE US HOPE AND
ENCOURAGEMENT AS WE WAIT PATIENTLY
FOR GOD'S PROMISES TO BE FULFILLED.
—ROMANS 15:4 NLT

· · · · · · · ·

God, when I'm sinking into discouragement, lift me up with the power of your Holy Spirit, who stirs faith and confidence in my heart. Amen.

Don't Ever Give Up

MAY YOU BE PREPARED TO ENDURE EVERY-
THING WITH PATIENCE, WHILE JOYFULLY
GIVING THANKS TO THE FATHER.
—COLOSSIANS 1:11–12 NRSV

Athletes do it. Missionaries do it. Servicemen and servicewomen do it. They endure hardships and make sacrifices because the prize they seek, the message they spread, and the values they fight for are worth it.

When we face a challenge that tests our patience and requires us to sacrifice our time and resources, we may wonder if we should continue. If we are serving a God-pleasing purpose, fulfilling a God-given duty, or struggling for a God-honoring cause, then we should not give up, but continue our good work.

God is the source of our willingness to endure, and wants us to do it with joy and patience.

I PRESS ON TO REACH THE END OF THE RACE
AND RECEIVE THE HEAVENLY PRIZE FOR WHICH
GOD, THROUGH CHRIST JESUS, IS CALLING US.
—PHILIPPIANS 3:14 NLT

God, it is a privilege to act as your heart and hands in this life. Grant me endurance so I may serve with pleasure. Amen.

When Enemies Roar

I WILL CALL UPON THE LORD, WHO IS WORTHY
TO BE PRAISED: SO SHALL I BE SAVED FROM
MINE ENEMIES. —PSALM 18:3 KJV

Most of us will never face military enemies on a battlefield. But we face other enemies every day—self-doubt, shame, isolation, or fear. God is just as interested in delivering us from these powerful enemies as he would be if we were facing an invading army.

God's method of rescue and restoration is somewhat different from a military encounter. He rebuilds us on the inside first, telling us the truth about who we are and how much we mean to him. The more he works with us, the more we live our lives with confidence and peace.

Those spiritual enemies that have stalked us can no longer keep us down.

HE DELIVERS ME FROM MY ENEMIES; SURELY
YOU LIFT ME ABOVE THOSE WHO RISE UP
AGAINST ME. —PSALM 18:48 NASB

God, thank you for driving out the enemies
in my life and for telling me the truth
about who I am. Amen.

Open My Eyes, Lord

I PRAY THAT THE EYES OF YOUR HEART
MAY BE ENLIGHTENED, SO THAT YOU WILL
KNOW WHAT IS THE HOPE OF HIS CALLING.
—EPHESIANS 1:18 NASB

Our God is a god of mystery, but only because in many ways we are unable to comprehend his greatness. In every way possible, he encourages us to know him personally.

He has given us the Bible, which is his own letter of introduction. In it we learn about his nature, his character, and his interaction with us from the very moment of creation. In addition, he sent us Jesus, his own beloved Son, to live among us and help us learn even more about him.

As you open your heart to God, he promises to open your eyes that you might know him better each day.

THERE WAS THE TRUE LIGHT WHICH, COMING
INTO THE WORLD, ENLIGHTENS EVERY MAN.
—JOHN 1:9 NASB

God, thank you for opening yourself to me, allowing
me to know you rather than just about you.
Thank you for calling me your friend. Amen.

Entering God's Kingdom

THE Lord YOUR GOD WILL BLESS YOU IN
THE LAND YOU ARE ENTERING TO POSSESS.
—DEUTERONOMY 30:16 NIV

*D*o I qualify? Am I good enough? If you have ever asked yourself whether you have what it takes to enter God's kingdom, his answer is no, you are definitely not good enough. None of us is.

The good news is that God, in the person of Jesus Christ, has qualified for us. Being without sin, the spotless Lamb of God offered his life for our salvation, our acceptance, and our forever in the presence of almighty God. Jesus is the only one good enough to have satisfied God, and he did that perfectly.

The kingdom of God is yours not because of your qualifications, but because of God's promise.

* * * * * * * *

IT IS YOUR FATHER'S GOOD PLEASURE TO
GIVE YOU THE KINGDOM. —LUKE 12:32 KJV

* * * * * * * *

God, thank you for sending your precious Son to make a way for me to enter your kingdom and to live in your presence forever. Amen.

Living Forever

I CAME SO THEY CAN HAVE REAL AND
ETERNAL LIFE, MORE AND BETTER LIFE THAN
THEY EVER DREAMED OF. —JOHN 10:10 MSG

Few if any of us want to spend all eternity strumming on harps and hopping from one fluffy white cloud to another. The cartoon versions of heaven are cute, but they aren't realistic. Heaven is the place where we truly come alive as God's children.

All the things we've hoped for—and more—are waiting for us there. The God who created us will welcome us there. Everything will be grander than we can now imagine, and we'll be reunited with loved ones, even some, perhaps, we've never met. Our eternal lifetime will be one of praise.

There simply isn't enough time in our earthly lifetime to know the full extent of God's love. That will take eternity.

THIS IS ETERNAL LIFE, THAT THEY MAY KNOW
YOU, THE ONLY TRUE GOD, AND JESUS CHRIST
WHOM YOU HAVE SENT. –JOHN 17:3 NASB

God, thank you for creating eternity so I can
get to know you, worship you, and take in
your great love for me. Amen.

In His Footsteps

IMITATE GOD, THEREFORE, IN EVERYTHING
YOU DO, BECAUSE YOU ARE HIS DEAR
CHILDREN. —EPHESIANS 5:1 NLT

With care, a little girl, barely old enough to walk, slipped her feet into her mother's shoes. She took a step, but her foot landed off center and the shoe flopped to the side. She took another step, and the second shoe fell off too. Everyone in the room watched as she straightened first one shoe and then the other before trying again.

On the next step, she fell, but she stood back up and gave it another go. Her determination to try again was fed by her desire to be like her mother, the one she loved.

We may falter when we seek to follow God's example, but God loves our efforts.

I'VE LAID DOWN A PATTERN FOR YOU. WHAT
I'VE DONE, YOU DO. —JOHN 13:15 MSG

God, I want to follow your example in everything I do. Thank you for teaching me as I grow in my knowledge of you. Amen.

Excellent Thoughts

IF THERE IS ANY EXCELLENCE AND IF THERE
IS ANYTHING WORTHY OF PRAISE, THINK
ABOUT THESE THINGS. —PHILIPPIANS 4:8 NRSV

What were you thinking?" It's a question we might ask when someone we love makes an ill-advised decision or falls into an avoidable predicament. We want to know what could have motivated their seemingly inexplicable course of action.

The thoughts we harbor and nurture affect how we see things, and how we see things affects how we do things. Faulty thinking can cause unnecessary fear and anxiety, and mean-spirited imaginings can poison our relationships.

God promises that when we offer our thoughts to him, he will help us keep them clean, wholesome, optimistic, and balanced, resulting in good words, actions, and outcomes. God promises we'll have lives worth living.

BE ALERT AND THINK STRAIGHT. –1 PETER 1:13 CEV

God, guard me against destructive thoughts. Let goodness, love, joy, optimism, and peace shape my thinking, words, and actions. Amen.

God's Promise

f Peace

THE MEEK SHALL INHERIT THE EARTH;
AND SHALL DELIGHT THEMSELVES IN THE
ABUNDANCE OF PEACE. —PSALM 37:11 KJV

Expect God's Best

THE EYES OF ALL LOOK EXPECTANTLY TO
YOU, AND YOU GIVE THEM THEIR FOOD IN
DUE SEASON. —PSALM 145:15 NKJV

We look for the best price in a store. We look for the best seat in a theater. We pick what we believe is the best choice from a menu. If we want the best, it's up to us to get it.

When it comes to our spiritual best, however, all we need to do is receive it. Why? Because God freely and generously gives it to us. We can expect forgiveness, compassion, joy, and peace of mind, because he promises those things. We can expect his wisdom to mark our way, because he said we can have it.

If you're looking for the best, expect it from God.

TO ALL WHO ARE THIRSTY I WILL GIVE FREELY
FROM THE SPRINGS OF THE WATER OF LIFE.
—REVELATION 21:6 NLT

God, immerse my heart and soul in all the best things you pour out on me to give my life meaning, purpose, and joy. Amen.

Settled in Faith

I LIVE BY FAITH IN THE SON OF GOD, WHO
LOVED ME AND GAVE HIMSELF FOR ME.
—GALATIANS 2:20 NIV

Even if we could constantly read the Bible and reflect on its words, we still would not have all the answers to our questions. Some concepts are too deep for human understanding, and others God chooses not to clarify.

This is where faith comes in—but what does that mean? It's not about saying the right words or thinking the right thoughts. It's about trusting the character and faithfulness of the person who has promised.

Having faith doesn't mean having all the answers. It means trusting in the one who knows every circumstance of our life. It means believing in and having confidence in the goodness of our God.

HAVE FAITH IN GOD. —MARK 11:22 NASB

God, I have placed my faith in you, no matter the circumstances or my inability to understand. Amen.

Great Is His Faithfulness

Today's upgrade arrives, and yesterday's tech device is out-of-date. New discoveries and fresh revelations are announced, and long-accepted concepts are replaced. Current opinions gain popularity, and time-honored beliefs and values seem hopelessly old-fashioned.

What a blessing to know that God's promises have remained intact and in force from the day they were first spoken, and they will remain valid to the end of time! God has not changed his mind on even one, and he has substituted no as-yet-unfulfilled promise with something else.

God is faithful to himself, and he is faithful to his word. You can depend on all God's promises today and forever.

●　●　●　●　●　●　●

I WILL PRAISE YOU FOR DOING THE WONDERFUL THINGS YOU HAD PLANNED AND PROMISED SINCE ANCIENT TIMES. —ISAIAH 25:1 CEV

●　●　●　●　●　●　●

God, when I wonder about any of your promises, remind me of your infinite faithfulness to all those who love you. Amen.

The Family of God

BOTH THE ONE WHO MAKES PEOPLE HOLY
AND THOSE WHO ARE MADE HOLY ARE OF
THE SAME FAMILY. —HEBREWS 2:11 NIV

We sometimes hear people refer to others as their "blood relatives." This simple term means that they are descendants of common ancestors; they share a bloodline.

When we are born into the family of God, we become his blood relatives. The blood that unites us is the blood Jesus shed on the cross, the blood that washes away our sins and makes us pure and holy in the sight of God.

The family of God is more than a whimsical, feel-good concept. It's grounded in blood, which is the essence of all life. No matter what happens, we are his.

WHOEVER DOES THE WILL OF MY FATHER IN
HEAVEN IS MY BROTHER AND SISTER AND
MOTHER. —MATTHEW 12:50 NIV

God, thank you for making us part
of your family through the blood of
Jesus, your Son. Amen.

Overcoming Fear

SAY TO THOSE WHO ARE OF A FEARFUL
HEART, "BE STRONG, DO NOT FEAR! HERE
IS YOUR GOD." —ISAIAH 35:4 NRSV

Fear can be paralyzing and disabling. But if we let him, God will meet us in our places of fear, and he will deliver us forever from this tyrant in our lives.

Perhaps you've seen a mother comfort her toddler who has been terrified by a large dog. Once the child knows his mother won't allow the dog to harm him, he probably breaks into a smile.

In the same way, God wants to set us free from all our fears. He wants to expose each fear for what it really is. He wants to leave us with nothing less than his perfect peace.

THERE IS NO FEAR IN LOVE; BUT PERFECT LOVE
CASTS OUT FEAR. —1 JOHN 4:18 NASB

God, when I am afraid, I will come to you. Thank you that you deliver me from all my fears. Amen.

Receive Forgiveness

LET IT BE KNOWN TO YOU, BRETHREN,
THAT THROUGH HIM FORGIVENESS OF SINS
IS PROCLAIMED TO YOU. —ACTS 13:38 NASB

Sin reveals weaknesses in our lives we would rather not own up to. Though we like to think of ourselves as good, kind, and loving, sometimes our words and actions betray us.

Throughout the Bible, God invites us to confess our failings, but we often sidestep his call. We might choose to deny our sinfulness, or even redefine wrongdoing as a personal choice or simple mistake. Yet when we take responsibility for our sinful thoughts and actions, God repeats his promise to forgive us and restore us to full relationship with him.

All we have to do is ask and open our hearts to receive it.

IF WE CLAIM TO BE WITHOUT SIN, WE DECEIVE
OURSELVES AND THE TRUTH IS NOT IN US.
—1 JOHN 1:8 NIV

God, open my eyes to the seriousness of my sins so that I can sincerely repent and receive the blessing of your forgiveness. Amen.

Basking in Freedom

THE LORD AND THE SPIRIT ARE ONE AND
THE SAME, AND THE LORD'S SPIRIT SETS US
FREE. —2 CORINTHIANS 3:17 CEV

The concept of freedom is that we are free to do things our own way. Too often, though, we end up pursuing one dream after another while failing to capture the pleasure, fulfillment, and peace of mind we crave.

God invites us to choose his way. He promises that when we follow his wisdom and counsel, we will not only find our freedom, but we will bask in it. As we permit him to turn our minds and hearts to the lives he has planned for us, deep satisfaction, spiritual serenity, and lasting contentment will be the result.

We are free to experience the joy he has prepared for us.

IF THE SON MAKES YOU FREE, YOU SHALL BE
FREE INDEED. —JOHN 8:36 NKJV

God, thank you for showing me that true freedom comes when I choose to become the person you created me to be. Amen.

All Things Are New

ANYONE WHO BELONGS TO CHRIST IS A NEW
PERSON. THE PAST IS FORGOTTEN, AND
EVERYTHING IS NEW. —2 CORINTHIANS 5:17 CEV

Beginnings are exciting—the first game of a tennis match, a wedding, the birth of a child, the start of a new job. No one knows what the future holds, because what's going to happen hasn't been written yet. Anything is possible.

Every day is a new beginning with God. Through his grace, forgiveness, and transforming power, God not only offers us a fresh start, but he also offers the promise that we'll become new people. Our mistakes, poor choices, and selfish desires are behind us. Who we are today begins a brand-new story—one filled with promise, potential, and purpose—cowritten by God, whose love for us will never fail.

I WILL GIVE YOU A NEW HEART AND PUT A
NEW SPIRIT WITHIN YOU. —EZEKIEL 36:26 NKJV

God, as I draw close to you, help me become
the person you created me to be. Amen.

The Closest of Friends

THERE IS A FRIEND WHO STICKS CLOSER
THAN A BROTHER. —PROVERBS 18:24 NKJV

Friends make a lot of promises. Yet even friends with the best intentions can't always keep the promises they make. Plans change. The unexpected happens. Miscommunication occurs.

Only one friend will always follow through. He holds fast to his promises, no matter what. God is a friend who's always by your side. He cheers you on when you're discouraged, draws you close when your heart breaks, and never rejects you, even if you turn away from him.

God understands what you want to say before you've thought or said a word, but he still longs to hear your voice. He truly is the best and most dependable friend you'll ever have.

I DON'T SPEAK TO YOU AS MY SERVANTS. I
SPEAK TO YOU AS MY FRIENDS. —JOHN 15:15 CEV

God, thank you for being my friend. Help me daily to be acutely aware of your loving and constant presence in my life. Amen.

A Bright Future

THINK OF THE BRIGHT FUTURE WAITING
FOR ALL THE FAMILIES OF HONEST AND
INNOCENT AND PEACE-LOVING PEOPLE.
—PSALM 37:37 CEV

Happily-ever-afters aren't reserved for fairy tales. Jesus' sacrificial death on the cross secured a victorious future for your personal story and invited you into a heavenly ever-after forever home.

But you don't have to wait until you go to heaven to enjoy a bright future. Every time you make a choice that honors God, you strengthen the foundation your tomorrows are built on. You'll still have troubles in your earthly life—hard times will be around as long as you live here. What God promises is peace and joy in him, regardless of circumstance. That's a terrific promise that will negate discouragement and fear.

GOOD PEOPLE CAN LOOK FORWARD TO
A BRIGHT FUTURE. —PROVERBS 13:9 NCV

God, anytime I begin to fear tomorrow,
please remind me of the victory you've
promised in the days to come. Amen.

God's Generosity

WHOEVER GIVES TO OTHERS WILL GET
RICHER; THOSE WHO HELP OTHERS WILL
THEMSELVES BE HELPED. —PROVERBS 11:25 NCV

We've been told that it is better to give than to receive. And what God promises us goes beyond that "better." He promises that when we give, we will receive.

From a mathematical perspective this makes no sense. If we subtract or divide our resources, we should have less, not more. But in God's economy, riches aren't measured on a balance sheet. They're eternal treasures of the heart.

Truly generous people don't try to use God's promise to their advantage. We don't give to receive. We give because there's a need—and God has met our needs with such generosity we're compelled to pass his provision on to others. Generosity is a never-ending circle of blessing.

* * * * * * *

* * * * * * *

God, help me hold loosely to the resources you've given me. Open my eyes to see a need, and show me how I can help meet that need. Amen.

Crowned with His Glory

YOU, O LORD, ARE A SHIELD ABOUT ME, MY
GLORY, AND THE ONE WHO LIFTS MY HEAD.
—PSALM 3:3 NASB

When we glorify God, we give him honor and praise. Since he created everything and is almighty, all-knowing, and eternal, this makes perfect sense. So, how—or why—would God bestow glory on us?

The glory we receive has nothing to do with worthiness and everything to do with proximity. When we walk close to God, we don't walk in his shadow. Instead we bask in his glory. His glory is reflected in us and through us. It's like donning a royal crown that was promised to us, a touchstone that reminds us and those around us that we're children of a glorious King.

· · · · · · · ·

WE ARE HAPPY BECAUSE OF THE HOPE WE HAVE OF SHARING GOD'S GLORY. —ROMANS 5:2 NCV

· · · · · · · ·

God, thank you for creating me in your image. Show me how to walk in a way worthy of your glory. Amen.

Taking Up the Calling

CONFIRM GOD'S INVITATION TO YOU, HIS
CHOICE OF YOU. DON'T PUT IT OFF; DO IT
NOW. DO THIS, AND YOU'LL HAVE YOUR
LIFE ON A FIRM FOOTING. —2 PETER 1:10 MSG

When your cell phone rings, you choose whether to answer it or not. The same is true when God calls. He invites you to draw near to him. He invites you to act on his behalf using your own unique gifts. He calls you to carry a message of hope to the world.

When you receive God's call, you needn't second-guess him by thinking you're not up to the task. God has a plan for you, and he already knows you have what it takes to do his will. He doesn't expect you to act on your own. He expects you to believe his promise that you can do everything through him.

FOR I CAN DO EVERYTHING THROUGH CHRIST,
WHO GIVES ME STRENGTH. —PHILIPPIANS 4:13 NLT

God, you've promised I can do all things through you. Give me the courage to respond to your call, trusting you for the victory. Amen.

He Is Faithful

THE Lord WILL KEEP ALL HIS PROMISES.
HE IS LOYAL TO ALL HE HAS MADE.
—PSALM 145:13 NCV

If God weren't faithful, it wouldn't matter what promises he made. We couldn't trust he would keep any of them.

Throughout history, however, God has proven to be true to his word. He promised consequences if Adam and Eve ate from a specific tree. And there were. He promised to send a Savior. And he did. He promised we'll spend eternity with him in heaven. And because God has proven faithful in the past, we can trust that we will.

God's faithfulness is the power behind his promises. We can rest in his promises. We have no need to question them. God has proven himself and his word to be steadfast and true.

YOUR STEADFAST LOVE IS HIGHER THAN THE
HEAVENS, AND YOUR FAITHFULNESS REACHES
TO THE CLOUDS. —PSALM 108:4 NRSV

God, help me become more aware of your
faithfulness in my life. I want to trust
you and your promises wholeheartedly.
Show me how. Amen.

God's Promise

of Faithfulness

HE WILL COVER YOU WITH HIS FEATHERS,
AND UNDER HIS WINGS YOU WILL FIND
REFUGE; HIS FAITHFULNESS WILL BE YOUR
SHIELD AND RAMPART. —PSALM 91:4 NIV

Completely Forgiven

LORD, YOU ARE KIND AND FORGIVING
AND HAVE GREAT LOVE FOR THOSE WHO
CALL TO YOU. —PSALM 86:5 NCV

It seems almost unfair to be asked to forgive someone who has hurt you deeply. It's as if you're saying that what happened doesn't matter. But that isn't true.

The Bible tells us every sin we've committed, whether big or small, is enough to sever our relationship with God. Yet God has forgiven every single one of our offenses. We have done plenty of things that hurt God, and even though we know we're guilty, God forgives us.

Our offenses have been covered by Jesus' death on the cross and his resurrection. May our gratitude for God's gift run as deep and true as his forgiveness. And may we find in our hearts the ability as well to forgive others.

YOU ARE A GOD OF FORGIVENESS, GRACIOUS AND
COMPASSIONATE, SLOW TO ANGER AND ABOUNDING
IN LOVINGKINDNESS. —NEHEMIAH 9:17 NASB

God, may I never forget the very high price
of your forgiveness. May my repentance be
my thank-you gift to you. Amen.

He Is Kind

LET, I PRAY, YOUR MERCIFUL KINDNESS BE
FOR MY COMFORT, ACCORDING TO YOUR
WORD TO YOUR SERVANT. —PSALM 119:76 NKJV

We're the children of an almighty God. Yet, our heavenly Father isn't only powerful; he's also kind. Not only is he alongside us in every battle we face, but he is also present in the quiet moments of ordinary days.

Perhaps God's kindness seems most apparent in details—when his Spirit buoys our hearts with an encouraging word, when his answer to an almost-forgotten prayer makes us smile, when an unexpected blessing provides much more than we need. God's quiet, inconspicuous kindness is simply one more way he reveals how much he cherishes us and how deeply he loves us.

THE MOUNTAINS SHALL DEPART, AND THE HILLS
BE REMOVED: BUT MY KINDNESS SHALL NOT
DEPART FROM THEE. —ISAIAH 54:10 KJV

God, you've promised to be kind,
as well as just, powerful, and strong.
Thank you for the many kindnesses you
bestow on me each day. Amen.

Unfailing Love

THE LORD's UNFAILING LOVE SURROUNDS THE
ONE WHO TRUSTS IN HIM. —PSALM 32:10 NIV

If you saw a movie where the leading male never let his beloved down, where he only spoke words that built her up, fulfilled his every promise, and unselfishly attended to her needs with a servant's heart, you'd say he was too good to be true. And you'd be right.

Only God is capable of perfect, unfailing love. That kind of love may feel rather far-fetched, since it's so far above anything we experience here on earth. It isn't that people don't love us, and love us well. Yet even so, on occasion their love will let us down. God's love never will. We're partnered in a divine relationship with him.

ABSOLUTELY *NOTHING* CAN GET BETWEEN US
AND GOD'S LOVE BECAUSE OF THE WAY THAT
JESUS OUR MASTER HAS EMBRACED US.
—ROMANS 8:39 MSG

God, thank you for loving me so perfectly,
when my own love so often falls short.
Teach me how to love more like you. Amen.

Showing Mercy

YOU SHOULD ALWAYS CLOTHE YOURSELVES
WITH MERCY, KINDNESS, HUMILITY, GENTLE-
NESS, AND PATIENCE. —COLOSSIANS 3:12 NCV

It seems that human beings are quick to judge and slow to show mercy. That seems to be our human nature. But something wonderful happens when God's Spirit comes to dwell within us. We become better people, not because God demands it, but because he has shown us mercy.

We never have to worry about coming before God and receiving a harsh sentence. If we are penitent, he promises us mercy, every time. As his beloved children, let us, too, offer mercy to those around us.

Let us also offer kindness, humility, gentleness, and patience, even to those who don't appear to deserve it. That's what God does for us.

BE MERCIFUL, JUST AS YOUR FATHER
IS MERCIFUL. —LUKE 6:36 NIV

God, your mercy is unending and undeserved. I never want to take it for granted. I am truly grateful for all that you do. Amen.

Never Alone

THE LORD IS NEAR TO THE BROKENHEARTED,
AND SAVES THE CRUSHED IN SPIRIT.
—PSALM 34:18 NRSV

Can you recall a time when you felt totally alone? Perhaps you moved to a new city and couldn't find even one familiar face at a social event. Or maybe you were grieving the loss of someone you dearly loved who journeyed to heaven before you. The next time you're feeling isolated, forgotten, or abandoned, take heart. You're not alone.

God is there. He'll never leave your side. That is the promise of the Holy Spirit. When you invite God into your life, he is there to stay. In good times, bad times, all the time, he is as close to you as your heartbeat, as close as your breath.

COME NEAR TO GOD, AND GOD WILL COME
NEAR TO YOU. —JAMES 4:8 NCV

God, thank you for remaining near, regardless of where I am or what I'm going through. Help me feel your closeness right now. Amen.

In His Presence

LET US COME BEFORE HIS PRESENCE WITH
THANKSGIVING, AND MAKE A JOYFUL NOISE
UNTO HIM WITH PSALMS. —PSALM 95:2 KJV

Usually we know when other people are around because we see them. We hear the sounds of voices and perhaps feel the touch of someone's hand. We know people are around us because our senses alert us and tell us it is so.

Being in God's presence is altogether different. We can't walk or drive somewhere to enter God's presence, because he is already with us. He dwells within us. When we cry out for help or offer a word of thanks, we're talking to God's indwelling presence. Even though our eyes, ears, and hands can't confirm that he's near, the Bible promises that God is with us.

MY PRESENCE SHALL GO WITH YOU, AND I WILL
GIVE YOU REST. —EXODUS 33:14 NASB

God, although I don't feel worthy of entering
your presence, I know your forgiveness, grace,
and love bid me "welcome" without reservation.

Thank you! Amen.

He Is Good

THE EARTH IS FULL OF THE GOODNESS OF
THE LORD. —PSALM 33:5 KJV

The Bible tells us that God is good. If we're honest
with ourselves, though, we know that there are
times when we have our doubts. The world around
us—and sometimes our life—is so broken and filled
with pain that we wonder how a good God could allow
such sorrow and misery.

In the same way that a parent's discipline or the
challenging words of a friend who sees our shortcom-
ings feel anything but good, our loving God promises
to always do what's best—even if it's hard or uncomfortable. God is our Father and our Friend. His actions
always reflect the goodness of his heart toward us.

TASTE AND SEE THAT THE Lord IS GOOD;
BLESSED IS THE ONE WHO TAKES REFUGE
IN HIM. —PSALM 34:8 NIV

God, thank you for promising to take
everything in our lives, even the hard parts,
and bring about something good. Amen.

Unending Grace

MY GRACE IS SUFFICIENT FOR YOU, FOR
POWER IS MADE PERFECT IN WEAKNESS.
—2 CORINTHIANS 12:9 NRSV

It's easy to be hard on ourselves. After all, there are
countless ways we can mess things up. We make mistakes, choose wrong roads, and even turn our backs on
those who love us, including God. That's why grace is
such a necessity in our lives.

Thankfully, God's reserve of grace is never exhausted.
Regardless of how many times we blow it, blame, condemnation, and punishment are not the main plot lines of our
life story. Grace is. We can't earn it and we don't deserve
it. All we can do is pass it on, as our gratitude for God's gift
inspires us to extend grace more freely to others.

HOW RICH IS GOD'S GRACE, WHICH HE
HAS GIVEN TO US SO FULLY AND FREELY.
—EPHESIANS 1:7–8 NCV

God, you've promised your grace
will never run out. Thank you! Your
grace gives me the freedom to move
forward without fear. Amen.

Suffering Loss

YOU WILL GRIEVE, BUT YOUR GRIEF WILL
TURN TO JOY. –JOHN 16:20 NIV

Life is a series of beginnings and endings. Unfortunately, many of those endings will break your heart—especially those that mark the end of a cherished relationship. The deeper the love, the deeper you feel the loss. Yet, love is worth the risk.

So is grief. Suffering a profound loss can change us. With God's help, it can uncover reserves of strength, wisdom, and faith we never realized were there. Like a mosaic, God promises to take the shattered pieces of our hearts and reassemble them in a beautiful, new way.

Like every work of art or heart, this takes time. But with God, the end results are always extraordinary.

YOU REMOVED MY SACKCLOTH AND CLOTHED
ME WITH JOY. —PSALM 30:11 NIV

God, I trust that you will fill my empty
places with your love. Help me move
forward in faith—and heal. Amen.

Lead Me, Lord

I HAVE SHOWN YOU THE WAY THAT MAKES SENSE; I HAVE GUIDED YOU ALONG THE RIGHT PATH. —PROVERBS 4:11 CEV

When it comes to hiking, a compass, maps, signs, and cairns can help keep us on the right path. However, when it comes to navigating rougher terrain, such as relationships, finances, and countless other situations we encounter on a regular basis, it's easy to get off track. We need God's guidance every day of our lives. Only when we allow his Word and his Spirit to lead us can we make the right choices in situations where the answer isn't easy to discern.

By staying connected with God through prayer, he promises to guide us through the complex maze of life.

I AM THE LORD YOUR GOD, WHO TEACHES YOU
WHAT IS BEST FOR YOU, WHO DIRECTS YOU IN
THE WAY YOU SHOULD GO. —ISAIAH 48:17 NIV

God, guide every decision I make, big or small.
Remind me to follow you and the Bible,
instead of following my own intuition. Amen.

God Takes Our Guilt

CREATE IN ME A PURE HEART, O GOD, AND
RENEW A STEADFAST SPIRIT WITHIN ME.
—PSALM 51:10 NIV

Guilt can be a positive thing. It's our body's way
of saying, "You've gone the wrong way. Hang a
U-turn!" Guilt can push us toward God, encourage us
to confess what we've done, and help detour us from
traveling that same wrong road in the future.

After we've been forgiven and have done all that's
in our power to set things right with God and others,
guilt has done its job. If we're still feeling guilty, something is amiss. If God doesn't condemn us, who are we
to continue to condemn ourselves?

Put your faith in God's promises and accept his
grace and forgiveness—completely.

TURN FROM EVIL AND DO GOOD, AND
YOU WILL LIVE IN THE LAND FOREVER.
—PSALM 37:27 NLT

God, help me recognize when feelings of guilt persist after you have forgiven me. Please help me release any false guilt I'm holding on to. Amen.

A Happy Heart

IF WE PLEASE GOD, HE WILL MAKE US
WISE, UNDERSTANDING, AND HAPPY.
—ECCLESIASTES 2:26 CEV

The pursuit of happiness is a national pastime. Yet, how can we successfully pursue something if we don't know where to find it? If we're looking for happiness, we should look to God.

As we draw close to him, our perspective shifts. We see things from an eternal point of view. We notice blessings we have been blind to in the past. We gain a better understanding of what truly satisfies and what is nothing more than a self-indulgent diversion.

Living in a way that pleases God will also please us. It changes us from the inside out. Instead of pursuing happiness, we'll find that we're carrying it around with us.

MAY THE RIGHTEOUS BE GLAD AND REJOICE
BEFORE GOD; MAY THEY BE HAPPY AND
JOYFUL. —PSALM 68:3 NIV

God, show me what I should wholeheartedly
pursue in this life. Make your desire
my heart's desire. Amen.

Safe in His Arms

I AM AN EXAMPLE TO MANY PEOPLE, BECAUSE
YOU ARE MY STRONG PROTECTION.
—PSALM 71:7 NCV

The world can be a dangerous place. All we have to do is watch the nightly news to know this, and yet, we don't need to walk around in fear. God walks with us, everywhere we go. God is ultimately in control, and he has promised us his protection. He has promised angels to surround us, his Spirit to guide us, and a safe haven in our heavenly home.

That doesn't mean nothing bad will ever happen to us. If we're facing danger, God holds us close. If escape isn't his plan, his peace and wisdom protect us in a different way. God provides what we need to face whatever comes our way.

DO NOT FEAR THOSE WHO KILL THE BODY BUT
CANNOT KILL THE SOUL. —MATTHEW 10:28 NKJV

God, may knowing that you're near and in control prevent me from fearing the future. I'm safe in your arms. Amen.

God's Healing Hands

I WILL RESTORE HEALTH TO YOU AND HEAL
YOU OF YOUR WOUNDS. —JEREMIAH 30:17 NKJV

God knows our bodies inside and out, from before we were born until now. He created us. He
knows how each bone fits together, how each organ
functions, and how many days each of our bodies will
live on this earth.

It is no surprise that one of God's names is the Great
Physician. Yes, we have doctors and nurses who help
us dramatically when we're ill. Ultimately, however,
healing lies in God's hands. Rather than relying solely
on finding the proper medication and physician to aid

our bodies when we're in ill health, it's good to know we can call on God.

God promises to heal us, body and soul.

• • • • • • • •

I AM THE LORD WHO HEALS YOU. —EXODUS 15:26 NKJV

• • • • • • • •

God, I know my healing is in your hands. If it's your will, may I be healthy and whole. Amen.

God's Promise

f Hope

YOU HAVE GIVEN ME HOPE. MY COMFORT
IN MY SUFFERING IS THIS: YOUR PROMISE
PRESERVES MY LIFE. —PSALM 119:49–50 NIV

The Blessing of Good Health

LIGHT IN A MESSENGER'S EYES BRINGS JOY
TO THE HEART, AND GOOD NEWS GIVES
HEALTH TO THE BONES. —PROVERBS 15:30 NIV

Good health is a wonderful gift, but it's also a gift
that is easy to take for granted. It's only when
our amazingly intricate bodies aren't functioning
at their best that we realize just how precious good
health is to us.

On the days when we feel strong, when we move
freely, see clearly, and hear the music of a friend's
laughter, we have an opportunity to pause and thank
God for our bodies. On the days when we struggle,

when we're weak or in pain, we can once again turn to our Creator, thank him for all he's given, and receive from him all that we need.

* * * * * * *

MY WHOLE BEING, PRAISE THE LORD AND DO NOT FORGET ALL HIS KINDNESSES. HE FORGIVES ALL MY SINS AND HEALS ALL MY DISEASES.
—PSALM 103:2–3 NCV

* * * * * * *

God, let me never take for granted the body you've given me. Help me to appreciate the body I have. Bless me with your gift of good health today. Amen.

Our Heavenly Home

HE PUTS A LITTLE OF HEAVEN IN OUR
HEARTS SO THAT WE'LL NEVER SETTLE
FOR LESS. —2 CORINTHIANS 5:5 MSG

There's no place like home, especially when the home we're referring to is heaven. The Bible describes heaven as paradise, a place with mansions and streets of gold. Whether this is an accurate depiction or a metaphor for something so wondrous we can't wrap our minds around it, we won't know until we get there.

What we do know is the Bible promises that a place has been prepared for each of us.

When life is hard and our hearts long for more, we're experiencing something akin to homesickness. One day that longing will end. We'll be home at last, with an eternity before us to enjoy and explore.

REJOICE AND BE GLAD, BECAUSE GREAT IS YOUR
REWARD IN HEAVEN. —MATTHEW 5:12 NIV

God, thank you for preparing a place for me.
I look forward to the day I share
that home with you. Amen.

He Hears Your Cry

OUR SOUL WAITS FOR THE Lord; HE IS OUR
HELP AND OUR SHIELD. —PSALM 33:20 NKJV

Even those who don't realize they're praying are likely to voice this universal cry in desperate times—"Help!"

God hears our cries for help. God is concerned about us, whether our need for help is a matter of everyday disappointment and feelings of defeat, or of a desperate matter of life and death. God's heart breaks in empathy when our hearts are broken. That's the nature of true love.

Never hesitate to call out to God. Like an emergency hotline, God's available 24 hours a day, 365 days a year. He offers more than just a listening ear. He also bestows peace, comfort, and wisdom during desperate times. He promises to hear and act.

I AM THE Lord YOUR GOD WHO TAKES HOLD OF
YOUR RIGHT HAND AND SAYS TO YOU, DO NOT
FEAR; I WILL HELP YOU. —ISAIAH 41:13 NIV

*God, may I never hesitate to cry out to you
when I'm in need. You're always near,
ready to act on my behalf. Amen.*

Created in Holiness

PUT ON YOUR NEW NATURE, CREATED
TO BE LIKE GOD—TRULY RIGHTEOUS AND
HOLY. —EPHESIANS 4:24 NLT

The word *holy* means "set apart." Like the good china, your best dress, or your heirloom tablecloth that only comes out at the holidays, you are special—set apart by God for finer things than living a life tainted by sin and discouragement.

We don't become holy by living a good life, trying to scrub our souls clean through penance or sacrifice. We become holy when we are set aside for God.

God alone has the power to make us holy. It's one more way we reflect his image. When we accept him as Lord, he promises to set us apart from who we once were and to make us his through and through.

NOW THAT YOU HAVE BEEN SET FREE FROM SIN
AND HAVE BECOME SLAVES OF GOD, THE BENEFIT
YOU REAP LEADS TO HOLINESS, AND THE RESULT
IS ETERNAL LIFE. —ROMANS 6:22 NIV

God, you are holy, set apart from everything you created. We are holy because we are yours. Thank you, Lord. Amen.

Receiving the Holy Spirit

YOU WILL RECEIVE POWER WHEN THE HOLY
SPIRIT HAS COME UPON YOU. —ACTS 1:8 NRSV

In the Old Testament, God bestowed his Spirit on
chosen individuals. Take King Saul, for example. At
one time, Saul was God's chosen ruler. But he fell out
of favor with the Lord when his impatience caused
him to lose his faith in God. God removed his Spirit
from Saul and bestowed it instead on David.

In the New Testament, God established a new covenant and a new promise. God promised his Spirit
would be a permanent gift to every individual who

believed in him. We are the blessed recipients of this promise.

From Pentecost on, God's presence and power have made a home in each one of his children.

* * * * * * *

THE SPIRIT IS GOD'S GUARANTEE THAT HE WILL GIVE US THE INHERITANCE HE PROMISED AND THAT HE HAS PURCHASED US TO BE HIS OWN PEOPLE. —EPHESIANS 1:14 NLT

* * * * * * *

God, thank you for the gift of your Holy Spirit. Help me to be more aware of your presence in my life every day. Amen.

Honesty before God

WHO MAY LIVE ON YOUR SACRED
MOUNTAIN? THE ONE . . . WHO SPEAKS THE
TRUTH FROM THEIR HEART. —PSALM 15:1–2 NIV

We can always rely on God's honesty. God is always honest with us. There will never be a well-constructed cover story or a fib to spare our feelings. God will always tell us the truth, and that's what he expects from us as well.

When we come before him, God wants honesty in our requests and in our worship. He also wants honesty in all our dealings with others. We need to abandon pretense and say exactly what we mean from our heart.

It's easy to speak honestly when we talk to God, when we tell him about all our troubles and problems. He knows us well and loves us much.

LET YOUR LOVINGKINDNESS AND YOUR TRUTH
CONTINUALLY PRESERVE ME. —PSALM 40:11 NKJV

God, shine a light on any areas of my life where I haven't been honest with you. Thank you for loving me despite my failings. Amen.

God Bestows Honor

RICHES AND HONOR ARE MINE TO GIVE.
SO ARE WEALTH AND LASTING SUCCESS.
—PROVERBS 8:18 NCV

God alone is truly worthy of honor. He's the only one who is perfect in love, integrity, and faithfulness. It only makes sense to say that he's the only one qualified to bestow honor on others. So it seems incomprehensible that he should choose to bestow honor on us.

When God deems us worthy of distinction and esteem, the only reason we merit such recognition is because of our relationship with him. His gift of honor is like a mirror, reflecting back to him what he's so graciously given us. It's like a king stooping down to honor his servant.

What a wonderful God we serve!

RICHES AND HONOR COME FROM YOU, AND
YOU RULE OVER ALL. —1 CHRONICLES 29:12 NRSV

God, it may sound silly to say I feel honored to be honored—but I am. It's all because of you. Amen.

Waiting in Hope

IT IS GOOD THAT ONE SHOULD HOPE AND
WAIT QUIETLY FOR THE SALVATION OF THE
LORD. —LAMENTATIONS 3:26 NKJV

Hope waits. It trusts something good is on the horizon. What we're hoping for may be out of sight or simply out of reach. Either way, hope trusts it's only a matter of time before God transforms that hope into reality.

What we hope for may not always look exactly like what God provides, but we can be confident God will provide just what we need. That's because at the heart of all our hopes is God himself. He's our creator, provider, sustainer, and redeemer.

One thing we never have to hope for is that God will keep his promises. God never fails to do what he says.

REST YOUR HOPE FULLY UPON THE GRACE THAT
IS TO BE BROUGHT TO YOU AT THE REVELATION
OF JESUS CHRIST. —1 PETER 1:13 NKJV

God, you know what I'm hoping for right now.
Please help my patience and trust grow
along with my love for you. Amen.

An Open Door

DO NOT NEGLECT TO SHOW HOSPITALITY
TO STRANGERS, FOR BY THIS SOME
HAVE ENTERTAINED ANGELS WITHOUT
KNOWING IT. —HEBREWS 13:2 NASB

The word *hospitality* can strike fear in the heart of those who feel ill-equipped to entertain. Yet God-centered hospitality doesn't require an immaculate home, gourmet cuisine, or conversational wit. When the Bible was written, being hospitable meant welcoming outsiders so cordially that those who were once strangers soon felt as though they belonged.

This kind of hospitality depends much more on opening your heart than your home. Every individual you encounter is someone God loves. As you look at others through God's eyes, you'll begin to see what you can do to make them feel welcome and the comfort of God's love.

Simply act on what you know to welcome former outsiders to feel comfort as insiders.

* * * * * * * *

SHARE WITH THE LORD'S PEOPLE WHO ARE IN NEED. PRACTICE HOSPITALITY. —ROMANS 12:13 NIV

* * * * * * * *

God, show me how to open the door of my heart, as well as my home, to those you lead me to love. Amen.

Walking Humbly

THIS IS THE ONE TO WHOM I WILL LOOK, TO
THE HUMBLE AND CONTRITE IN SPIRIT, WHO
TREMBLES AT MY WORD. —ISAIAH 66:2 NRSV

Humility fits like a perfect pair of shoes. It's seeing ourselves as God does, having an accurate self-image that's not too big or too small, but fits just right. There's no place for an overinflated ego or underdeveloped sense of self-worth in God's kingdom. Yes, we're irreplaceable and uniquely gifted, but we're fallible. We're fragile and resilient, but also forgiven. We are beloved children of an almighty Father.

Holding on to the truth about the strengths and weaknesses that comprise each one of us is the key to walking humbly with God. Only through his promise of strength and grace can we become all he created us to be.

THE REWARD FOR HUMILITY AND FEAR OF
THE Lord IS RICHES AND HONOR AND LIFE.
—PROVERBS 22:4 NRSV

*God, thank you for loving me as I am,
and promising to help me mature, bringing
out your best in me. Amen.*

Spiritual Hunger

BLESSED ARE THOSE WHO HUNGER AND
THIRST FOR RIGHTEOUSNESS, FOR THEY
WILL BE FILLED. —MATTHEW 5:6 NRSV

We don't always recognize hunger for what it is. We may feel light-headed, headachy, or lethargic, but we don't need aspirin or a catnap. We need food. It's the only thing that will satisfy physical hunger.

Likewise, we don't always recognize our hunger for God. We may feel discontented, melancholy, or anxious, as if we're running on empty. Trying to quell this type of hunger with entertainment, activity, or a holiday will offer only temporary relief.

God has promised to satisfy our hunger for him. When we look for peace and purpose in a world of chaos and confusion, he is the one to whom we can turn.

I AM THE BREAD OF LIFE. HE WHO COMES TO
ME SHALL NEVER HUNGER. —JOHN 6:35 NKJV

God, you've promised to satisfy my hunger
for you. Remind me to reach out to you through
reading the Bible every day. Amen.

Who Are You?

LIVE OUT YOUR GOD-CREATED IDENTITY.
—MATTHEW 5:48 MSG

If someone asks you who you are, you can state your name or occupation. You can mention who you are in relation to others, such as son or daughter, spouse, widow, parent. You could affirm that you are a child of God. Labels like these help others better understand our place in this world, but they don't paint a full picture of who we are.

Our identity is as distinctive as our fingerprint. God designed us that way. We're more than a label. We're individuals, one-of-a-kind creations.

Perhaps God is the only one who knows our true identity—everything we are today and have the promise to become tomorrow.

GOD'S SPIRIT TOUCHES OUR SPIRITS
AND CONFIRMS WHO WE REALLY ARE.
—ROMANS 8:16 MSG

God, help me better understand who you created me to be and to live my life in a way that best reflects my true identity. Amen.

Inspiration from Above

ALL SCRIPTURE IS GOD-BREATHED AND
IS USEFUL FOR TEACHING, REBUKING,
CORRECTING AND TRAINING IN
RIGHTEOUSNESS. —2 TIMOTHY 3:16 NIV

A lighthouse guides and warns ships at sea. The Bible is like a lighthouse. It points us in a favorable direction. Depending on the trustworthiness of the Bible means that we can trust its inspiration to go where it leads. We choose whether we'll follow that guiding light or chart a different course.

We can be inspired by the words, works, and lives of those we admire. The most trustworthy and beneficial inspiration comes from God himself. God's character, the Bible, and his Spirit are the most positive influences we can find in this world.

God has promised to inspire the course we chart for our lives.

* * * * * * * *

EVERYTHING I WILL SAY IS TRUE AND SINCERE, JUST AS SURELY AS THE SPIRIT OF GOD ALL-POWERFUL GAVE ME THE BREATH OF LIFE. —JOB 33:2–4 CEV

* * * * * * * *

God, you inspire me on so many levels. Thank you for promising to make your chosen path clear for me. Amen.

Listen Up

SENSIBLE INSTRUCTION IS A LIFE-GIVING
FOUNTAIN THAT HELPS YOU ESCAPE ALL
DEADLY TRAPS. —PROVERBS 13:14 CEV

You order a new bookcase online. When it arrives, you notice those dreaded words: SOME ASSEMBLY REQUIRED. Inside the box you find forty-seven individual pieces and a ten-page instruction booklet. What should you do? Read the instructions.

Building a life is much more complex than building a bookcase. That's why God has given us instructions to help us along the way.

Those instructions can be found in places like the Bible, Sunday's message at your local church, and the wise words and actions of God-followers all over the world. Every day there are new lessons to learn. We must look for them, listen to them, and apply them to our lives.

GIVE INSTRUCTION TO A WISE MAN, AND HE
WILL BE STILL WISER; TEACH A JUST MAN, AND
HE WILL INCREASE IN LEARNING.
—PROVERBS 9:9 NKJV

God, help me to listen closely for and
apply all the lessons you want me
to learn today. Amen.

God's Promise

of Kindness

WITH EVERLASTING KINDNESS I WILL HAVE
COMPASSION ON YOU. —ISAIAH 54:8 NIV

Doing What Is Right

YOU UPHOLD ME IN MY INTEGRITY, AND
SET ME BEFORE YOUR FACE FOREVER.
—PSALM 41:12 NKJV

When we say a building has integrity, we mean it's in perfect alignment, standing solid on its foundation. The same could be said of us when integrity is a cornerstone of our lives.

When our character, plans, and purpose are founded on the immovable rock of God and the Bible, our words and actions align more closely with God's will. God not only promises countless benefits to those who walk in integrity, but he also promises to help us avoid the sinking sand of our emotions and desires.

God shows us the way, helps us stay on track, and rewards us abundantly for every good choice.

THE INTEGRITY OF THE HONEST KEEPS
THEM ON TRACK. —PROVERBS 11:3 MSG

God, please reveal any cracks in my integrity.
I want to align my life more closely with
you and the Bible. Amen.

Never-Ending Joy

MAY THE GOD OF HOPE FILL YOU WITH
ALL JOY AND PEACE IN BELIEVING.
—ROMANS 15:13 NRSV

A well-known traditional Christmas carol declares "Joy to the world! The Lord is come." The day that our all-powerful God bundled himself up in an infant's body and came to earth was cause for incredible joy. But the song, the story, and our joy don't stop there.

The lyrics continue, "Let earth receive her King; let every heart prepare him room." Jesus did more than enter the realm of humanity. He came to enter every individual heart. When we invite him in as Lord and King, he remains with us.

His Spirit encourages us, guides us, and holds us close—a source of joy that never runs dry.

RESTORE TO ME THE JOY OF YOUR SALVATION,
AND SUSTAIN IN ME A WILLING SPIRIT.

—PSALM 51:12 NRSV

God, show me how to delight even more
deeply in you. You are my deepest,
most constant source of joy. Amen.

No Fear of Judgment

THE JUDGMENTS OF THE Lord ARE TRUE:
THEY ARE COMPLETELY RIGHT. —PSALM 19:9 NCV

A *judgment* is a judicial ruling that requires payment of some sort. Payment can often be made with cash, community service, or incarceration in a correctional facility. Sometimes, the debt is so egregious that the offender's own life is legally required as payment.

God's judgment against us is too big ever to repay. Even sacrificing our own lives couldn't compensate for the countless times and ways we've rebelled against God. But we don't need to fear God's judgment or future punishment. When God promised that his Son's sacrifice paid our debt in full, he meant it.

God doesn't hold so much as a grudge against us. He holds us close in love.

LET MY JUDGMENT COME FORTH FROM YOUR PRESENCE; LET YOUR EYES LOOK WITH EQUITY.
—PSALM 17:2 NASB

God, you know everything I've done, but I never need to fear you. My debt is paid, thanks to you. Hallelujah! Amen.

Tempered by Mercy

I AM THE LORD, WHO EXERCISES KINDNESS,
JUSTICE AND RIGHTEOUSNESS ON EARTH,
FOR IN THESE I DELIGHT. —JEREMIAH 9:24 NIV

If another driver hits your car, your home is burglarized, or someone you love is injured by a doctor's negligence, you want justice. However, if the responsibility for an accident or poor decision falls on you, you don't want justice. What you want is mercy.

How blessed we are that our God is more than just. He is also kind and merciful.

He doesn't turn a blind eye to what we've done or afford us a bit of wiggle room when it comes to his laws. He knows right from wrong better than anyone. Yet, he has promised that mercy, rather than legalism, will be the law by which he judges us.

SUNRISE BREAKS THROUGH THE DARKNESS
FOR GOOD PEOPLE—GOD'S GRACE AND MERCY
AND JUSTICE! —PSALM 112:4 MSG

God, teach me how to temper my own sense
of justice with grace when it comes to dealing
with those who have offended me. Amen.

Jesus Tipped the Scales

SINCE WE HAVE BEEN MADE RIGHT WITH
GOD BY OUR FAITH, WE HAVE PEACE
WITH GOD. —ROMANS 5:1 NCV

The statue of Lady Justice stands in courthouses around the world. She is often depicted wearing a blindfold to show her objectivity and impartiality. She holds the scales of justice in one hand (weighing the evidence) and a sword in the other (symbolizing power).

God is not Lady Justice. Although he holds ultimate power, his love and grace have cancelled out any impartiality. As for the evidence, Jesus has tipped the scales in our favor. The only evidence God sees when he looks at us is that Jesus has paid for our sins. Case closed. We have been justified, set free by God's love and grace—his unmerited favor.

* * * * * * *

THROUGH ONE MAN'S RIGHTEOUS ACT THE FREE GIFT CAME TO ALL MEN, RESULTING IN JUSTIFICATION OF LIFE. –ROMANS 5:18 NKJV

* * * * * * *

God, standing justified before you humbles me. May I never take Jesus' sacrifice for granted. Thank you for your love, forgiveness, and grace. Amen.

A Gentle Touch

BE KINDLY AFFECTIONATE TO ONE ANOTHER
WITH BROTHERLY LOVE, IN HONOR GIVING
PREFERENCE TO ONE ANOTHER.
—ROMANS 12:10 NKJV

Kindness isn't a necessity. We can feed the hungry, care for the sick, and clothe the poor without it. Yet when kindness accompanies a gift of service, it underscores the worth of the person who receives it. It's like a card accompanying a gift that reads, "You matter to God and to me. Your physical needs are important, and so is your heart."

Little things mean a lot. A smile, a hug, a willingness to listen to someone, even when that person's actual needs remain verbally unexpressed, that's kindness in action.

God promises to be kindhearted with us. What an honor it is to bless others with that same tender love.

DO NOT LET KINDNESS AND TRUTH
LEAVE YOU; BIND THEM AROUND YOUR
NECK, WRITE THEM ON THE TABLET OF
YOUR HEART. —PROVERBS 3:3 NASB

God, help me to love others well not only by serving them diligently, but also serving them with patience, kindness, and sincerity. Amen.

Living in the Kingdom

THE KINGDOM OF GOD IS NOT JUST A LOT
OF TALK: IT IS LIVING BY GOD'S POWER.
—1 CORINTHIANS 4:20 NLT

Our arrival in heaven awaits us in the future, but God's kingdom is at hand right here and now. Since God's own Spirit is alive within us, his kingdom is active wherever and whenever we share his love.

As we allow God to guide us and work through us, his kingdom expands around the globe.

Wherever we Christians reside, God's presence and power become more evident to those around us. Through our prayers, our words, and our actions, we help God's heavenly kingdom come to our earthly home.

YOUR KINGDOM COME, YOUR WILL BE DONE, ON
EARTH AS IT IS IN HEAVEN. —MATTHEW 6:10 NASB

God, help me spread your love and your message of hope wherever I go so that your kingdom may become more visible in this world. Amen.

Seeking Knowledge

GRACE AND PEACE BE YOURS IN ABUNDANCE
THROUGH THE KNOWLEDGE OF GOD AND OF
JESUS OUR LORD. —2 PETER 1:2 NIV

Life is too short, and our finite brains too limited, to know everything there is to know about God. But just because we can't know it all, it doesn't mean we shouldn't strive to know as much as we can. The more we learn about God, the more reasons we discover to love, worship, honor, obey, and trust him.

It helps to read the Bible and to study it. It helps to get involved in a Bible study with fellow believers. We are encouraged to pray for wisdom about how to apply the knowledge we receive.

God promises that if we seek him, we'll find him. What greater pursuit could there be?

THE LORD GRANTS WISDOM! FROM HIS MOUTH
COME KNOWLEDGE AND UNDERSTANDING.
—PROVERBS 2:6 NLT

God, lead me toward knowledge that matters. Instead of facts and figures, help fill my mind with the knowledge of who you are. Amen.

Into God's Hands

WE ARE THE CLAY, YOU ARE THE POTTER;
WE ARE ALL THE WORK OF YOUR HAND.
—ISAIAH 64:8 NIV

The Bible compares each of us to a piece of pottery being shaped by an almighty Potter. Unlike traditional pottery, however, we have free will. We can wriggle right down off that potter's wheel and insist on doing things our way. If we do that, however, it never ends well.

God knows best where we need to be made strong or tender, whether we need to speak up or remain silent, wait patiently or move forward in hope.

Only when we let go of our own self-centered strategy for life, can God shape us into the work of art he had in mind the day he fashioned us in our mother's womb.

THE CLAY DOES NOT ASK THE POTTER, "WHAT ARE YOU DOING?" THE THING THAT IS MADE DOESN'T SAY TO ITS MAKER, "YOU HAVE NO HANDS." —ISAIAH 45:9 NCV

God, shape me into the person you want me to be, according to your promise. Help me honor you with my life and my words. Amen.

Living in Him

THE LIFE OF EVERY LIVING THING IS IN HIS HAND, AND THE BREATH OF EVERY HUMAN BEING. —JOB 12:10 NLT

Every breath is a gift. On difficult days, when each breath is heavy with sorrow or racked with pain, God promises that his presence and power are still within reach. And on those glorious days, the ones filled with so much love, joy, and wonder that we never want them to end, God's Spirit dances with us.

Life is an adventurous, unpredictable journey. Nevertheless, it is easy to fall into ruts of habit and predictability, taking the gift of our life for granted. May we be aware today of how even the most ordinary moments hold glimpses of God's extraordinary hand.

Let us return to him the gift of our thanks and praise.

THE Lord GOD TOOK DUST FROM THE GROUND
AND FORMED A MAN FROM IT. HE BREATHED THE
BREATH OF LIFE INTO THE MAN'S NOSE, AND THE
MAN BECAME A LIVING PERSON. —GENESIS 2:7 NCV

God, thank you for this life. Help my
gratitude grow with every year you so
graciously bring my way. Amen.

Light My Way

THE Lord IS MY LIGHT AND MY SALVATION;
WHOM SHALL I FEAR? —PSALM 27:1 KJV

When the electricity goes out, we lose perspective. We hesitantly feel our way around in the dark, bumping our toes into things we'd safely walk around if the lights were on. Even in a familiar room, we feel a bit lost, unsure, and perhaps even afraid.

Without God's guiding light, life can feel like a dark room. In contrast, when we lean on God's Spirit and the Bible, we clearly see what's ahead of us, instead of fearing what our imagination says may be hiding in the dark.

As long as we stay close to God, he promises his light will never go out in our lives.

I AM THE LIGHT FOR THE WORLD! FOLLOW ME, AND YOU WON'T BE WALKING IN THE DARK. YOU WILL HAVE THE LIGHT THAT GIVES LIFE.

—JOHN 8:12 CEV

God, you're my eternal source of wisdom, guidance, clarity, and power. Thank you for lighting the proper path I should travel. Amen.

God's Promise

of Patience

> FOR THIS REASON I FOUND MERCY, SO THAT
> IN ME AS THE FOREMOST [SINNER], JESUS
> CHRIST MIGHT DEMONSTRATE HIS PERFECT
> PATIENCE AS AN EXAMPLE FOR THOSE WHO
> WOULD BELIEVE IN HIM FOR ETERNAL LIFE.
> —1 TIMOTHY 1:16 NASB

No, Never Alone

I AM CONTINUALLY WITH YOU; YOU HOLD
ME BY MY RIGHT HAND. —PSALM 73:23 NKJV

Just because we feel lonely doesn't mean we are
alone. Even when it looks like we're the only one in
the room, God promises he's there with us. There will be
times, though, when we need companionship, conversation, or a warm hug. God has placed that longing in us
as well. He wants us to reach out to his other children.

When we feel that way, we can ask God to bring to
mind others who may need our companionship. Then,
we pray for the courage to connect by text, phone call,
email, or in person and start up a conversation.

When we alleviate someone else's loneliness, we
almost always alleviate our own.

LET'S AGREE TO USE ALL OUR ENERGY IN
GETTING ALONG WITH EACH OTHER. HELP
OTHERS WITH ENCOURAGING WORDS.
—ROMANS 14:19 MSG

God, please provide the energy and resolve
I need to reach out to others when I feel alone.
Thanks for being here with me. Amen.

Only for You

AS THE DEER PANTS FOR THE WATER
BROOKS, SO MY SOUL PANTS FOR YOU,
O GOD. —PSALM 42:1 NASB

Our bodies can't survive long without food or water. God hardwired our bodies to remind us of that fact. When we're hungry, our stomachs gurgle and rumble. When we're thirsty, our throats grow parched and our thinking becomes fuzzy. Our bodies communicate what is needed in tangible ways.

In the same way, God calls us to communion with him. When our souls hunger for his presence, we can easily confuse that longing with feelings of discontent, melancholy, or apathy. But God promises that when we turn our thoughts to him, that longing will be fulfilled.

God keeps close to us and desires that we keep close to him.

I'M HOMESICK—LONGING FOR YOUR SALVATION;
I'M WAITING FOR YOUR WORD OF HOPE. MY
EYES GROW HEAVY WATCHING FOR SOME SIGN
OF YOUR PROMISE. —PSALM 119:81 MSG

God, even when I'm unaware of it, I know my soul longs for you. Teach me how to draw closer to you each day. Amen.

Open Hearts

MAY MERCY, PEACE, AND LOVE BE YOURS
IN ABUNDANCE. —JUDE 2 NRSV

We may "fall" in love, but to continue loving over time takes hard work. Consider Jesus. Think of all he sacrificed because of his deep love for us. We never know when our love for another will call us to the point of sacrifice. Yet love is worth it. Our hearts know it.

Whether it's for our spouse, our child, a dear friend, or even a total stranger who's in need—we feel the pull of love. It's the pull to do something to lift others up, to shower them with the love God's showered on us.

Loving others is as much a joy as being loved in return.

A NEW COMMANDMENT I GIVE TO YOU,
THAT YOU LOVE ONE ANOTHER, EVEN AS
I HAVE LOVED YOU, THAT YOU ALSO LOVE
ONE ANOTHER. —JOHN 13:34 NASB

God, show me how to give and accept love.
Allow your love to freely flow through my
life and into the lives of others. Amen.

One before God

TWO ARE BETTER THAN ONE, BECAUSE THEY
HAVE A GOOD REWARD FOR THEIR TOIL.
—ECCLESIASTES 4:9 NRSV

Marriage is a flesh-and-blood illustration of the intimate relationship God shares with us. However, when mortal men and women live out this illustration side by side over the years, the picture they paint with their relationship isn't always an accurate or flattering "holy" one.

Having two flawed individuals promise to love each other under any and every circumstance is bound to have its ups and downs. A God-centered marriage, however, is made up of three persons, not two.

When a husband and wife join their lives to each other and to God, God promises that love truly can conquer all with the help of humility, servanthood, and grace.

* * * * * * *

MARRIAGE IS TO BE HELD IN HONOR
AMONG ALL. —HEBREWS 13:4 NASB

* * * * * * *

God, help me never take my marriage for granted. Keep my heart tender toward my spouse, ready to serve, encourage, forgive, and love. Amen.

Growing Up

SOLID FOOD IS FOR THE MATURE, WHO BY
CONSTANT USE HAVE TRAINED THEMSELVES
TO DISTINGUISH GOOD FROM EVIL.
—HEBREWS 5:14 NIV

You may have put your school days behind you
years ago, but you haven't stopped learning.
You're still discovering new things, increasing in
knowledge, gaining experience, and honing skills.

In spiritual matters, too, you haven't stopped
learning. At first, there was a desire to discover who
God is and what he says. Then, as understanding
increased, so did your capacity to delve deeper into
the life-changing mysteries of God. Spiritual growth

continues to come as you apply what you know to your life. You have the word of the Bible on it.

God's Spirit will work in your heart, mind, and soul to support you as you keep learning and keep growing in faith.

* * * * * * *

GROW IN THE GRACE AND KNOWLEDGE
OF OUR LORD AND SAVIOR JESUS CHRIST.
—2 PETER 3:18 NIV

* * * * * * *

God, I want to know more about you. Teach me your truths so I may grow in spiritual knowledge and understanding. Amen.

Think on This

O HOW LOVE I THY LAW! IT IS MY MEDITATION
ALL THE DAY. —PSALM 119:97 KJV

Sh! Being quiet is the prerequisite to meditation. A few minutes of quiet reflection opens your heart and soul to receive God's message of comfort, hope, and love.

Begin by silencing distractions, such as the TV and other electronic devices. Leave your cell phone in the other room. Next, sit comfortably and set aside the day's problems—don't worry, they won't go away. Finally, re-call or read a Bible verse, and prepare to listen.

Focused only on God as he is revealed in the Bible, you may discover a deeper meaning or a fresh insight. Even better, you may realize a practical way to apply the Bible to your life. Meditation is listening to God.

BE STILL, AND KNOW THAT I AM GOD.
—PSALM 46:10 KJV

God, increase my desire to sit quietly in your presence. Open my ears so that I may hear everything you want to say to me. Amen.

Looking Up

SURELY GOODNESS AND MERCY SHALL
FOLLOW ME ALL THE DAYS OF MY LIFE.
—PSALM 23:6 NRSV

Today, the act of showing mercy is often associated with extreme circumstances. A merciful judge lightens a harsh sentence, for instance. Merciful people provide practical help to those less fortunate than themselves. In God's eyes, however, all of us need his mercy. Not one among us can claim the obedience God expects or the holiness he requires. Yet rather than turn his back on us, God extends mercy. He readily forgives the penitent heart and gently guides the teachable soul to follow in his ways.

Because of God's mercy, the burden of guilt is lifted, the offense of sin is forgiven, and the light of his love is assured.

HIS MERCY EXTENDS TO THOSE WHO FEAR HIM,
FROM GENERATION TO GENERATION. —LUKE 1:50 NIV

God, thank you for being merciful to me,
despite all I have said and done. Thank you
for your ever-merciful love. Amen.

Right Thinking

I WILL PUT MY LAW IN THEIR MINDS
AND WRITE IT ON THEIR HEARTS.
—JEREMIAH 31:33 NIV

You can't see the rudder on a boat crossing a lake, but you can know how the rudder is set by the direction the vessel is headed. Similarly, your thoughts aren't visible to others, but your words and actions are clues to what you must be thinking.

Harsh, bitter thoughts generate squalls of angry words and outbursts of hostile behavior. Gentle and joyful thoughts brighten your mood, smooth your words, and strengthen your ability to cope with whatever the day brings.

If you don't like where you're headed today, check your thoughts. Make sure your behavioral rudder is set in the direction you want to go.

* * * * * * *

WHATEVER IS TRUE, WHATEVER IS NOBLE, WHATEVER IS RIGHT, WHATEVER IS PURE, WHATEVER IS LOVELY, WHATEVER IS ADMIRABLE . . . THINK ABOUT SUCH THINGS. —PHILIPPIANS 4:8 NIV

* * * * * * *

God, infuse my mind and heart with thoughts of peace, joy, compassion, understanding, and love for you and for others. Amen.

Signs and Wonders

HE PERFORMS WONDERS THAT CANNOT
BE FATHOMED, MIRACLES THAT CANNOT
BE COUNTED. —JOB 5:9 NIV

You've heard about miracles performed, or maybe you've even witnessed a miracle. But the biggest of these awe-inspiring events is the miracle of God's love for the world. Think about it.

God the Father created the universe and everything in it from nothing.

Jesus Christ, the Son of God, was born true God and true man, and he brought salvation to all who believe in him.

The Holy Spirit enlightens minds and hearts so all may discover the joy of a close relationship with him.

Christianity is a study in miracles. God's promises hold true, his compassion continues, his presence remains. God's love for us is an ongoing, joy-filled, day-to-day miracle.

WITH GOD ALL THINGS ARE POSSIBLE.
—MATTHEW 19:26 NIV

God, let me never forget the wonder of creation, of love, and of life. In all, help me to see and to rejoice in the miracle. Amen.

Living for Others

SURELY THE LORD YOUR GOD HAS BLESSED
YOU IN ALL YOUR UNDERTAKINGS.
—DEUTERONOMY 2:7 NRSV

When you're on a mission, you have a goal in mind. Your mission might be to reach a destination, complete a project, or master a skill. As a believer, you are on the most important mission of all, and that is to discern, to embrace, and to do God's will.

Generally, God's will is evident. Simply look at your God-given responsibilities. Though some responsibilities undoubtedly bring you joy and satisfaction, others may require patience, persistence, generosity, and selflessness. This is all part of your mission!

Each day, rely on God's strength. When he gives you a mission, he also gives you everything you need to make it happen.

COMMIT YOUR ACTIONS TO THE LORD, AND YOUR
PLANS WILL SUCCEED. —PROVERBS 16:3 NLT

God, whenever I feel weak and overwhelmed,
turn my heart and mind to you, the source of
my strength and power. Amen.

Deep and Wide

I KNOW ALL THE BIRDS OF THE MOUNTAINS,
AND THE WILD BEASTS OF THE FIELD ARE
MINE. —PSALM 50:11 NKJV

What can compare with the splendor of a sunset or the rhythm of waves stroking the sand? Who wouldn't smile to catch a snowflake or savor the fragrance of a rose? The gifts of nature delight heart and soul.

As with any gift, nature has a giver—God. He created everything in nature, from minuscule grains of sand to massive clusters of stars. Wherever you find it, nature reminds you of God's creative power, assures you of his loving presence, and speaks to you of his divine sovereignty.

Look at the sky. Touch a flower. Give thanks to God, because these are among his magnificent gifts to you.

THE HEAVENS PROCLAIM THE GLORY OF GOD.
THE SKIES DISPLAY HIS CRAFTSMANSHIP.
—PSALM 19:1 NLT

God, let the beauty of nature fill my heart with joy, praise, wonder, and gratitude for all you have made. Amen.

Love and Obedience

THE PROOF THAT WE LOVE GOD COMES
WHEN WE KEEP HIS COMMANDMENTS AND
THEY ARE NOT AT ALL TROUBLESOME.
—1 JOHN 5:3 MSG

In his 1929 book of essays, *The Thing*, G. K. Chesterton wrote, "Don't ever take a fence down until you know the reason why it was put up." What does that mean? If you don't know the reason the fence was built, then you can't know if it is no longer needed. The same is true for God's commandments.

God forbids murder, stealing, lying, and cheating. Okay, we understand. But what about all the rest? Are they irrelevant today? No. Those who choose to tear down the "fence" may simply not understand why God has erected it.

What might seem to be an illogical limitation may actually be his love separating you from danger.

God, help me to take all your commandments seriously, even those that I don't understand or the ones that others choose to ignore. Amen.

Waiting on the Lord

IF WE HOPE FOR WHAT WE DO NOT SEE, WE
WAIT FOR IT WITH PATIENCE. —ROMANS 8:25 NRSV

Online retailers scramble for more ways to get you
what you want as soon as they possibly can. You
can even order merchandise and have it at your door-
step within an hour!

While it's exciting to receive products so quickly,
most things in life take time. A crop needs seasons of
rain and sunshine before it's ready for harvest. Wisdom
requires decades of personal experience and reflection
before it's mature. Faith compels us to walk at a steady
pace as it becomes a firm source of strength.

Remember, the sweetest fruit ripens slowly. Be patient with yourself—and with God.

BE STILL BEFORE THE Lord, AND WAIT
PATIENTLY FOR HIM. —PSALM 37:7 NRSV

God, don't let me give up, but help me
practice patience as I learn and grow in faith
and in love for others. Amen.

Seeking Peace

SINCE WE ARE JUSTIFIED BY FAITH, WE
HAVE PEACE WITH GOD THROUGH OUR
LORD JESUS CHRIST. —ROMANS 5:1 NRSV

Even if no bullets ricochet off walls, no explosions shake the ground, no arguments strain relations, still there is no peace. Peace—genuine, lasting peace—does not depend on what happens around you. Rather, peace depends on what goes on inside you.

God invites you to enjoy his peace. Jesus offers complete forgiveness to you, quieting an accusing conscience. His Spirit strengthens faith inside you, giving you the ability to withstand attacks of doubt and despair. His love comforts you when worry strikes or when you are harmed by the wrongdoing of others.

Throughout all the days of your life, God promises to be there for you. Rely on him. Receive his peace.

DON'T LET YOUR HEARTS BE TROUBLED. TRUST
IN GOD, AND TRUST ALSO IN ME. —JOHN 14:1 NLT

God, when trouble surrounds me, help me
reach out to you for the kind of peace this
world can never provide. Amen.

Able under Fire

MOMENTARY, LIGHT AFFLICTION IS PRO-
DUCING FOR US AN ETERNAL WEIGHT OF
GLORY FAR BEYOND ALL COMPARISON.
—2 CORINTHIANS 4:17 NASB

It is no secret. As a believer in Jesus Christ, you're going to suffer persecution, which could range from dismissive words to raw prejudice.

The Bible speaks about the persecution believers endure because of their belief in Jesus. We are reminded that we have a glorious future ahead of us, and that we possess his strength and comfort today. Through the work of his Spirit in us, God enables us not only to remain firm in our faith but also to extend forgiveness to those who harass us.

A Christ-filled loving response in the face of persecution will highlight the reality of God's presence in our lives.

LOVE YOUR ENEMIES AND PRAY FOR THOSE
WHO PERSECUTE YOU, SO THAT YOU MAY BE
CHILDREN OF YOUR FATHER IN HEAVEN.
—MATTHEW 5:44–45 NRSV

God, whenever I am harassed because
of my faith in your presence and
promises, help me respond with kindness,
compassion, and love. Amen.

Stay with the Plan

BE ALERT SERVANTS OF THE MASTER,
CHEERFULLY EXPECTANT. DON'T QUIT IN
HARD TIMES; PRAY ALL THE HARDER.
—ROMANS 12:12 MSG

Time and effort go into any worthwhile project. Say we hope to play the piano well, become an expert cook, or develop a winning computer program. Before we reach any goal, we have to spend countless hours and overcome multiple obstacles.

A meaningful spiritual life doesn't come instantly either. As we embrace a relationship with God, we're likely to come up against periods of apathy and boredom. At times, we might feel too busy to focus on spiritual truths. But these feelings are all part of reaching spiritual maturity.

If we stay with the plan, God promises us a deeper, richer, and more vibrant spiritual life.

* * * * * * *

IF YOU SEEK HIM, HE WILL BE FOUND BY YOU.
—1 CHRONICLES 28:9 NIV

* * * * * * *

God, when I get tired and want to give up, strengthen my determination to know you better and grow in spiritual maturity. Amen.

He Alone Matters

WITHOUT FAITH NO ONE CAN PLEASE GOD.
WE MUST BELIEVE THAT GOD IS REAL
AND THAT HE REWARDS EVERYONE WHO
SEARCHES FOR HIM. —HEBREWS 11:6 CEV

Genuine gifts have no strings attached. Sincere
compliments come from the heart. True service
is given without the expectation of a return, because
anything else is only skin deep.

But genuine gifts do have a return to you. Faith
gives substance to what you do for others. The time, effort, and resources you share with those in need, motivated by faith, please God. Your words of prayer and
praise, springing from faith, are acts of worship to

God. Your daily actions, performed because of faith, honor God. When God alone is your reason, God rewards.

Why you are doing what you do is so much more important to God than what you are doing.

* * * * * * * *

THE LORD DOES NOT LOOK AT THE THINGS
PEOPLE LOOK AT. PEOPLE LOOK AT THE OUTWARD
APPEARANCE, BUT THE LORD LOOKS AT THE HEART.
—1 SAMUEL 16:7 NIV

* * * * * * * *

God, let everything I do for others come from a heart centered in faith. Help me to focus all I do on you. Amen.

God's Promise

of Goodness

SURELY YOUR GOODNESS AND LOVE WILL
FOLLOW ME ALL THE DAYS OF MY LIFE, AND
I WILL DWELL IN THE HOUSE OF THE LORD
FOREVER. —PSALM 23:6 NIV

God of Power

WITH GOD'S POWER WORKING IN US, GOD
CAN DO MUCH, MUCH MORE THAN ANYTHING
WE CAN ASK OR IMAGINE. —EPHESIANS 3:20 NCV

When you take your desires to God, what do you expect? Some people anticipate little or nothing, while others demand that God give them exactly what they have asked for. God does neither. Instead, he gives bigger and better than anyone can imagine.

God might withhold something from you because he has a better idea in mind. He might not act according to your specifications because he knows another way, a way opening you to receive greater gifts and blessings. Perhaps you can't think of anything that could possibly match, much less top, your request, but God can.

Ask. Pray. But remember, the God of immense power will answer.

WITH GOD NOTHING SHALL BE IMPOSSIBLE.
—LUKE 1:37 KJV

God, help me to trust you completely, for you have the will and the power to work in my life in big ways. Amen.

Praise Him

I SHALL YET PRAISE HIM, WHO IS THE HEALTH
OF MY COUNTENANCE, AND MY GOD.
—PSALM 43:5 KJV

When couples speak the traditional wedding
vows, they promise to love and cherish each
other "for better for worse, for richer for poorer, in
sickness and in health." Similarly, your relationship
with God compels you to love him by praising him in
all situations.

Praise comes easily when everything goes your
way. You are aware of God's presence, you appreciate
his goodness, and you feel strong in faith and love for
others. But if your mind clouds with doubt, your heart
turns heavy with grief, or your circumstances bring

one trouble after another, praise becomes difficult. Nevertheless, praise is still essential.

At all times, praise him—not because God needs it, but because love requires it.

. . . .

LET US BE GLAD AND REJOICE, AND LET US GIVE HONOR TO HIM. —REVELATION 19:7 NLT

. . . .

God, plant in me the kind of faith that loves you, thanks you, and praises you in all circumstances of life. Amen.

He Hears Us

THE EYES OF THE LORD WATCH OVER THOSE
WHO DO RIGHT, AND HIS EARS ARE OPEN
TO THEIR PRAYERS. —1 PETER 3:12 NLT

Have you ever had the experience of being so close in a loving relationship with someone that you knew what he or she was going to say before it was said? Yet you wouldn't want the talking to stop. Because of love, you're always glad to listen.

God's intense love is the reason that he invites you to talk to him. Of course he knows what you need, what you want, and what you plan to say. Yet daily conversation nurtures your relationship with him, just as it does with another person.

A conversation between you and God alone is your time to speak and his time to delight in the sound of your voice.

CALL TO ME AND I WILL ANSWER YOU.

—JEREMIAH 33:3 MSG

God, thank you for inviting me to pray. Thank you for promising to hear my prayers and to answer them according to your love. Amen.

Pride in Our God

OUR PRIDE IS IN THE NAME OF THE LORD
OUR GOD. . . . WE SHALL RISE AND STAND
UPRIGHT. —PSALM 20:7–8 NRSV

Pride sometimes requires action. Pride in your family and pride in your nation prompt you to defend them, and pride in your abilities compels you to use them for your benefit and for the good of others.

Pride in God is no less energetic. It means you deliberately shun whatever would belittle his name and wholeheartedly embrace all that honors and praises him. Because of your pride in him as your Lord and Savior, you pray for the strength and the will to stand up for your faith whenever necessary.

Be proud, and let it show. Take active, purposeful, God-pleasing pride in being who—and whose—you are.

I AM NOT ASHAMED! I KNOW THE ONE I HAVE
FAITH IN. —2 TIMOTHY 1:12 CEV

God, let my pride in you lead me to obey
your commandments and honor you in the
things I do and say. Amen.

Prospering His Way

WHOEVER PURSUES RIGHTEOUSNESS
AND LOVE FINDS LIFE, PROSPERITY AND
HONOR. —PROVERBS 21:21 NIV

Not even the most prudent financial planning on your part guarantees wealth. Certainly, wise money management significantly improves the likelihood of future well-being, but it cannot promise it.

Your way to spiritual prosperity, however, comes with a guarantee—God's guarantee. As you study and reflect on his messages to you in Scripture, your understanding steadily increases, your confidence continues to grow, and your power to resist temptation progressively strengthens over time. Every act of obedience out of love for God rewards you with freedom from the poverty of guilt and regret.

God promises you a prosperous and honorable life when you seek righteousness and love.

* * * * * * * *

STOCKPILE TREASURE IN HEAVEN, WHERE IT'S SAFE FROM MOTH AND RUST AND BURGLARS.
—MATTHEW 6:20 MSG

* * * * * * * *

God, set my mind and heart on that which will bring me lasting joy, genuine peace, and a closer walk with you. Amen.

The Price of Protection

YOU ARE MY HIDING PLACE! YOU PROTECT
ME FROM TROUBLE, AND YOU PUT SONGS
IN MY HEART. —PSALM 32:7 CEV

In some parts of our larger cities, business owners
pay premiums to demanding criminals to ensure
that their businesses are not robbed or burglarized, in
most cases by the criminals themselves. This unjust
extortion tax is called "protection."

When God promises to protect us, his children, he demands nothing in return. Instead, he watches over us as
a father watches over his own precious children. His angels are always on duty, taking on all purveyors of evil.

God knows that we may not always pause to thank
him for his protection. But when we do, our offering is
pure and unsolicited, and it delights his heart.

THE LORD WILL PROTECT YOU FROM ALL
DANGERS; HE WILL GUARD YOUR LIFE. THE LORD
WILL GUARD YOU AS YOU COME AND GO, BOTH
NOW AND FOREVER. —PSALM 121:7–8 NCV

God, thank you for the assurance that we
are never alone, but rather we always are
under your watchful eye. Amen.

All Our Needs

MY GOD WILL FULLY SATISFY EVERY NEED OF
YOURS ACCORDING TO HIS RICHES IN GLORY
IN CHRIST JESUS. —PHILIPPIANS 4:19 NRSV

God provides for both body and soul. He sees to our physical needs by blessing us with abilities and opportunities that enable us to earn our livelihood. Usually we're able not only to see to our needs and the needs of our family, but also to share with those who must rely on the compassion and generosity of others.

To meet our spiritual needs, God has given us the Bible so we can learn about him and heighten our awareness of his presence. In addition, he sends his Spirit into our hearts to nurture our faith and strengthen our trust in him.

There's always plenty when God is the provider.

GENEROUS TO A FAULT, YOU LAVISH YOUR FAVOR
ON ALL CREATURES. —PSALM 145:16 MSG

God, all that I have comes from your hands.
Thank you for providing me with everything
I need for body and soul. Amen.

Pure and Healthy

GOD BLESSES THOSE PEOPLE WHOSE HEARTS
ARE PURE. THEY WILL SEE HIM!
—MATTHEW 5:8 CEV

We take care of our bodies by watching what goes into our mouths. We might avoid foods that have little nutritional value, and those that aren't conducive to good health. Certainly we wouldn't think of eating anything that might poison us.

Good spiritual health works in a similar way. We build, maintain, and nourish our souls by feeding them with the Bible and other God-honoring input. We stay away from damaging activities, places, ideas, and people that might sicken and poison our spiritual lives.

God has promised to help us discern the good from the bad, so that our thoughts and our souls will remain healthy and pure.

CREATE PURE THOUGHTS IN ME AND MAKE ME FAITHFUL AGAIN. —PSALM 51:10 CEV

God, immerse my heart and mind in those things that nourish my soul with goodness, kindness, purity, and love. Amen.

For His Purpose

TO EVERYTHING THERE IS A SEASON, A TIME
FOR EVERY PURPOSE UNDER HEAVEN.
—ECCLESIASTES 3:1 NKJV

"Why am I here?" That question continues to engage thinkers, and you can find a myriad of human-deduced answers out there.

If you want to know the real reason, however, ask the one who created you. In the Bible, God says that who you are and where you are happened by design, not by chance. Even if you're in an unhappy place right now, he promises to use it to his good purpose—perhaps to build you up in strength and perseverance, reveal to you his life-giving power, or deepen your insight and experience.

He has given you life, and where there is everlasting life, there is purpose.

IN HIM WE LIVE, AND MOVE, AND HAVE
OUR BEING. —ACTS 17:28 KJV

God, open my eyes to perceive the plans you
have in mind for me, because in your purpose
rests my fulfillment and joy. Amen.

Joyful Reconciliation

WE ALSO REJOICE IN GOD THROUGH
OUR LORD JESUS CHRIST, THROUGH
WHOM WE HAVE NOW RECEIVED THE
RECONCILIATION. —ROMANS 5:11 NKJV

An argument erupted between you and a loved one. Later, the spiteful words exchanged were not forgotten, and resentment built up on both sides.

You regret what happened, so you call to apologize. You hear similar words on the other end of the line, and the two of you forgive each other from the heart. The relationship is restored, and now you are at peace.

The burden of guilt is like a rift between friends. It chills your relationship with God.

Yet God has already called you, offering his forgiveness. It is reconciliation with him that brings lasting joy and genuine peace.

ALL THINGS ARE OF GOD, WHO HAS
RECONCILED US TO HIMSELF THROUGH
JESUS CHRIST. –2 CORINTHIANS 5:18 NKJV

God, thank you for reaching out to me and initiating reconciliation between us. I want to be in relationship with you. Amen.

Redeemed by Love

PUT YOUR HOPE IN THE Lord, FOR WITH THE Lord IS UNFAILING LOVE AND WITH HIM IS FULL REDEMPTION. —PSALM 130:7 NIV

If anyone asks you why you believe you are going to heaven, you can answer with one word: *love*. It's the overwhelming, all-encompassing, and infinitely active love of Jesus that led you to accept your full and complete redemption.

His promise that he has done everything needed for your heavenly tomorrow frees you to reflect his love by doing earthly good for others. With no anxiety about your future, you can immerse yourself in today's blessings, beauty, discoveries, and opportunities to serve others.

You may not be able to explain the depth of his redeeming love, but you can joyfully believe it, live it, and share it.

IN HIM WE HAVE REDEMPTION THROUGH HIS
BLOOD, THE FORGIVENESS OF OUR TRESPASSES,
ACCORDING TO THE RICHES OF HIS GRACE.
—EPHESIANS 1:7 NASB

God, thank you for your redemptive love that
I can joyfully express to others in the things
I do and say. Amen.

Those Who Come Near

FRIENDS LOVE THROUGH ALL KINDS OF
WEATHER, AND FAMILIES STICK TOGETHER IN
ALL KINDS OF TROUBLE. —PROVERBS 17:17 MSG

In folklore as in movies, the heroes are those who single-handedly fight the dragon and win the battle. In real life, however, no one person does it all.

Our ability to give and receive help builds relationships. Trust grows as we learn that family and friends will come through for us, and fulfillment is ours as we discover the satisfaction of being there for our loved ones.

Even the most self-sufficient person needs the strengths and capabilities, the support and encouragement, and the closeness and confidences of other people.

God often keeps his promises to us through the people in our lives.

＊ ＊ ＊ ＊ ＊ ＊ ＊ ＊

NO ONE HAS GREATER LOVE THAN THIS, TO
LAY DOWN ONE'S LIFE FOR ONE'S FRIENDS.
—JOHN 15:13 NRSV

＊ ＊ ＊ ＊ ＊ ＊ ＊ ＊

God, grant me the humility to accept help from others, and grant me the willingness to reach out to them in their time of need. Amen.

A Good Name

A GOOD REPUTATION AND RESPECT ARE
WORTH MUCH MORE THAN SILVER AND
GOLD. —PROVERBS 22:1 CEV

If you take identity theft seriously, you do everything you can to guard against it. But do you make a similar effort to protect your reputation?

How you speak, act, and interact with family, friends, and associates determines the kind of reputation you will gain. Even when you've established a good reputation, it must be maintained or it could crumble in a single moment by the revelation of scandal, cover-up, or offensive conduct.

Protect your good reputation every day by speaking kindly and courteously in all situations, by doing the right thing even when you're inconvenienced, and by giving others the regard you desire for yourself. God promises that by so doing you will gain respect.

* * * * * * * *

LIVE A QUIET LIFE, MINDING YOUR OWN BUSINESS AND WORKING WITH YOUR HANDS. . . . THEN PEOPLE WHO ARE NOT BELIEVERS WILL RESPECT THE WAY YOU LIVE. —1 THESSALONIANS 4:11–12 NLT

* * * * * * * *

God, help me to choose each day to live a life that is worthy of you. May I honor you in everything I do and say. Amen.

True Sorrow

GODLY SORROW BRINGS REPENTANCE
THAT LEADS TO SALVATION AND LEAVES
NO REGRET. —2 CORINTHIANS 7:10 NIV

Genuine repentance is more than saying "I'm sorry." Unless those words are followed by a change in behavior, any apology rings hollow.

God always welcomes your sorrowful heart, no matter what has caused its burden. He has promised his comfort and forgiveness, and more. He has promised the gift of his Holy Spirit to strengthen you and help you avoid wrong words and actions in the future. Yet even if you must return to God weighed down by the same sorrow, your sincere repentance invites his Spirit to lift you up again.

Anyone might feel sorry, but true sorrow is marked by an earnest desire to make a significant, God-motivated change, and God will honor it.

STOP SINNING AND TURN TO GOD! THEN PROVE WHAT YOU HAVE DONE BY THE WAY YOU LIVE. —ACTS 26:20 CEV

God, thank you for the assurance of your forgiveness. Send your Spirit into my heart so I may live a life of true repentance. Amen.

God's Promise

f Gentleness

TAKE MY YOKE UPON YOU, AND LEARN FROM ME; FOR I AM GENTLE AND HUMBLE IN HEART, AND YOU WILL FIND REST FOR YOUR SOULS.
—MATTHEW 11:29 NRSV

Stepping Up

THE LAST AND FINAL WORD IS THIS:
FEAR GOD. DO WHAT HE TELLS YOU.
—ECCLESIASTES 12:13 MSG

As in any family, our God has established certain rules of conduct, which he expects his children to obey. Some see this as God's way of bullying and controlling. But that could not be further from the truth.

Careful examination of God's commandments reveals that they are protective in nature. God wants to spare us the misery and destruction that come with certain thoughts and actions. He promises that when we behave responsibly concerning his commandments, our lives will draw good things to us—love, joy, peace, and abundance, to name just a few.

God always looks after our best interests.

IF YOU LISTEN TO THESE REGULATIONS AND FAITH-
FULLY OBEY THEM, THE LORD YOUR GOD WILL KEEP
HIS COVENANT OF UNFAILING LOVE WITH YOU, AS
HE PROMISED. —DEUTERONOMY 7:12 NLT

God, thank you for always looking out for me and for helping me to make choices that will bring good things to my life. Amen.

Resting in Him

COME TO ME, ALL OF YOU WHO ARE WEARY
AND CARRY HEAVY BURDENS, AND I WILL
GIVE YOU REST. —MATTHEW 11:28 NLT

Imagine picking up a box and stumbling under its weight. Now a friend much stronger than you are comes along and says, "Here, let me take that." Immediately the load is lifted from your arms and you sigh with relief. But after a few minutes, you yank the box from your friend and start struggling again.

God invites you to unload the full weight of your fears, troubles, and worries on him. But when you do it, don't take it back! Instead, face forward with confidence, assured that things will work out for you.

His strength is yours. Rely on the promise of his power, resting at ease in him.

LET MY SOUL BE AT REST AGAIN, FOR THE
LORD HAS BEEN GOOD TO ME. —PSALM 116:7 NLT

God, let me give you and leave with you all that burdens my heart so I may walk with serenity wherever you lead. Amen.

To Live Again

YOU WILL RESTORE MY LIFE AGAIN; FROM
THE DEPTHS OF THE EARTH YOU WILL
AGAIN BRING ME UP. —PSALM 71:20 NIV

The one we loved is gone, the job we depended on is no longer ours, the doctor's diagnosis is serious. Our world has crumbled, and it's hard to imagine anything but tears.

Yet God reaches out to us with comfort and peace. In the bleakest circumstances, his Spirit reminds us of God's promise to remain with us, console us, and strengthen us. He invites us to stay close to him, trusting and hoping in him as he shows us our world made new.

There is nothing broken that God cannot put back together, nothing lost that he cannot restore. In his time and according to his will, he will do it.

YOU WILL HAVE PAIN, BUT YOUR PAIN WILL
TURN INTO JOY. —JOHN 16:20 NRSV

God, when my dreams shatter, grant me
the peace and comfort you promise to all
who put their trust in you. Amen.

Newness of Life

CHRIST WAS RAISED FROM THE DEAD BY THE
GLORY OF THE FATHER, SO WE TOO MIGHT
WALK IN NEWNESS OF LIFE. —ROMANS 6:4 NRSV

Physical death can strike suddenly, but spiritual death takes place over time. There are signals, such as indifference to what God has to say, lack of effort to pray and connect with God, and choices contrary to his will. You have the ability to recognize these signs in others and in yourself.

God desires only healthy spiritual growth for everyone. Where he finds inner apathy, he sends his Spirit to reenergize faith and revitalize commitment to his way. He calls, invites, and incites the heart to be open to his influence and power.

If you see the signs, pray. Pray for what he longs to give: newness of life.

THE WORDS THAT I HAVE SPOKEN TO YOU
ARE SPIRIT AND LIFE. –JOHN 6:63 NRSV

God, wherever I discover signs of spiritual decline, turn my heart and mind immediately to you, the sole source of life. Amen.

Spiritual Eyes

HE REVEALS DEEP AND HIDDEN THINGS; HE
KNOWS WHAT IS IN THE DARKNESS, AND
LIGHT DWELLS WITH HIM. —DANIEL 2:22 NRSV

Some corrective eye surgeries take weeks or maybe even months to heal. Recovering patients often receive their sight gradually, as shadows dissipate and vision is restored.

As God works on your spiritual eyesight, keener vision comes with time. God promises that your perception of spiritual truths will sharpen as you get to know him better. Perhaps now there are concepts in Scripture that you find puzzling, but meaning and purpose will take shape as you continue to reflect, pray, and apply the Bible to your life.

Like your physical eyes, your spiritual eyes are precious—entrust them to no one but the one who can give you genuine spiritual vision.

* * * * * * *

KEEP YOUR EYES ON JESUS, WHO BOTH BEGAN AND FINISHED THIS RACE WE'RE IN. —HEBREWS 12:2 MSG

* * * * * * *

God, sharpen my spiritual vision and light the way ahead as I continue to meditate on your deep and profound truths. Amen.

The Lord Gives

THE LORD REWARDS PEOPLE WHO ARE FAITH-
FUL AND LIVE RIGHT. —1 SAMUEL 26:23 CEV

Have you thought, "What's in it for me if I have a relationship with God?" In the Bible, God answers before you have a chance to ask.

God promises to give his unconditional love to all who come to him. That means there are no prerequisites, no tests, no qualifications you must meet before he receives you with open arms. His forgiveness, compassion, help, strength, and salvation are as readily available to the "good" as well as the "bad" among us, to the conventional as well as to the unconventional, to the lifelong worshiper as well as the newly repentant soul.

God rewards our faith abundantly, and there's everything in it for you.

DO NOT, THEREFORE, ABANDON THAT CONFIDENCE
OF YOURS: IT BRINGS A GREAT REWARD.
—HEBREWS 10:35 NRSV

God, thank you for the great gifts you shower on me when I joyfully walk in relationship with you and honor your ways. Amen.

Living for Jesus

CAST YOUR CARES ON THE LORD AND HE
WILL SUSTAIN YOU; HE WILL NEVER LET THE
RIGHTEOUS BE SHAKEN. —PSALM 55:22 NIV

Perhaps you can recall a time when your intervention defused an argument, or your timely help eased another's pain. Even if no one gave you credit, you still felt good about yourself for doing what you did.

Your willingness to go with God's desires rather than your own offers the same good feeling. When you know you're doing the right thing, it doesn't matter whether others see and approve. It's nice when it happens, of course, but what's important is knowing you are walking in his way.

God promises that when we live for him, he will bestow on us God-given confidence, conviction, and peace of mind.

GOOD PEOPLE WILL KEEP ON DOING RIGHT,
AND GOD'S PEOPLE WILL ALWAYS BE HOLY.
—REVELATION 22:11 CEV

God, never let me get tired of doing what you
would have me to do, even if others
never notice or seem to care. Amen.

Giving It All

OUR SACRIFICE IS TO KEEP OFFERING
PRAISE TO GOD IN THE NAME OF JESUS.
—HEBREWS 13:15 CEV

One definition of the word *sacrifice* is "to give up something valuable for a better cause, a greater good." That might mean giving up a vacation to save for college or giving of our time to help others. Sacrifice, at least in this context, is a function of will.

When Jesus gave his life for us, it was of his own choosing. He left his exalted seat at the right hand of God his Father, in order to bring erring mankind back into his Father's eternal family. This was no simple transaction; it was a costly sacrifice.

Our sacrifice should be to demonstrate that his sacrifice was not in vain.

THOSE WHO TRY TO HOLD ON TO THEIR LIVES
WILL GIVE UP TRUE LIFE. THOSE WHO GIVE
UP THEIR LIVES FOR ME WILL HOLD ON TO
TRUE LIFE. —MATTHEW 10:39 NCV

God, thank you for choosing to give your life
for mine. I will honor that sacrifice by
always remembering and celebrating
what you did for me. Amen.

Rescue Me

SURELY GOD IS MY SALVATION: I WILL TRUST,
AND WILL NOT BE AFRAID. —ISAIAH 12:2 NRSV

Your faith in Jesus' sacrifice for your sin brings you his promise of salvation from sin's penalties and his promise of eternal life, but that's not all.

Faith saves you from feelings of powerlessness, because you know you possess his strength. It keeps you from fearing the future, because you're confident that no matter what happens, God will be with you. Faith holds temptation and harmful influences at bay, because your heart and mind are focused on God's will.

Your faith in Jesus saves you right now—for a life driven by meaning and purpose, filled with thankfulness and praise, and rich in joy and peace.

THE LORD IS MY STRENGTH AND SONG, AND IS
BECOME MY SALVATION. —PSALM 118:14 KJV

God, thank you for the gift of your Son,
Jesus Christ, whose life, death,
and resurrection made salvation and
eternal life possible for me. Amen.

Real Satisfaction

HE HAS SATISFIED THE THIRSTY SOUL,
AND THE HUNGRY SOUL HE HAS FILLED
WITH WHAT IS GOOD. —PSALM 107:9 NASB

We see a product we would like to have. Even though it costs more than we should spend, we buy it. *Because after I get this,* we say to ourselves, *I'll be satisfied.* Trouble is, we're satisfied only until the next appealing product appears!

Lasting satisfaction comes when we permit God to give us those things that are worth our time and attention, such as moderation, contentment, humility, simple pleasures, and self-control. He loads us up with love, joy, and peace. Then he fills us with desire to share what we have with others.

God promises us satisfaction that lasts, and it's free.

I SATISFY THE WEARY ONES AND REFRESH EVERY-
ONE WHO LANGUISHES. —JEREMIAH 31:25 NASB

God, set my heart and mind on those things you alone can give, things that will fill me with lasting satisfaction. Amen.

Living in God's Word

USING THE SCRIPTURES, THE PERSON WHO
SERVES GOD WILL BE CAPABLE, HAVING
ALL THAT IS NEEDED TO DO EVERY GOOD
WORK. —2 TIMOTHY 3:17 NCV

GOD DOESN'T CALL THE EQUIPPED, a church sign reads, HE EQUIPS THE CALLED. Your interest in learning about him means that he is calling you. Now expect to be equipped!

In Scripture, God lays out for you everything you need to know about him—his relationship with you and his plan of salvation. He clearly states his commandments, and provides many examples of his presence in the lives of ordinary men, women, and children. He generously pours out words of encouragement, inspiration, reassurance, and, most of all, enduring love.

When you are living in and according to the Bible, you are equipped for life today and every day.

＊ ＊ ＊ ＊ ＊ ＊ ＊

MAN SHALL NOT LIVE BY BREAD ALONE, BUT BY EVERY WORD THAT PROCEEDS FROM THE MOUTH OF GOD. —MATTHEW 4:4 NKJV

＊ ＊ ＊ ＊ ＊ ＊ ＊

God, equip me with your words and promises in Scripture so that I can do everything you have called me to do. Amen.

Reaching Out to God

SEARCH FOR THE Lᴏʀᴅ AND FOR HIS STRENGTH;
CONTINUALLY SEEK HIM. —PSALM 105:4 ɴʟᴛ

It feels as if you're doing all the work, right? You're
reflecting on Scripture, taking time for prayer, and
applying God's guidelines to your daily life.

Yet it is God who first reached out to you. He put in
place a plan for your redemption, a promise fulfilled in
the person of Jesus Christ. Through Jesus' death and
resurrection from death, you receive his promise of
forgiveness from all sin. God keeps on reaching out as
his Spirit stirs your heart and soul to a strong, mature
relationship with him.

Keep reaching out to God—and take delight in knowing that he first reached out to you.

WE LOVE HIM, BECAUSE HE FIRST LOVED US.
—1 JOHN 4:19 KJV

God, thank you for reaching out to me with your goodness, forgiveness, compassion, and love. Let me always reach out to you! Amen.

Serving God

RENDER SERVICE WITH ENTHUSIASM, AS TO
THE LORD AND NOT TO MEN AND WOMEN.
—EPHESIANS 6:7 NRSV

The sixteenth-century bishop Saint Francis de
Sales noted that "there is nothing small in the
service of God." His observation reminds us that no
matter how low or high our God-given responsibilities rank in the eyes of the world, we are serving God
when we serve others.

In God's sight, telling one child about God's love and
ministering to an entire congregation are no different.
Greeting each customer with a smile at the grocery
checkout and making fair and honest decisions in the
corporate boardroom are equally important.

Whether we're in the public eye or working largely unnoticed by others, we serve God when our words and actions reflect his love and promises.

. . . .

THERE ARE DIFFERENT KINDS OF SERVICE,
BUT THE SAME LORD. —1 CORINTHIANS 12:5 NIV

. . . .

God, as I go about my daily work, let me never forget that I am not merely doing a job, but I am serving you. Amen.

Joy for Sorrow

GLADNESS AND JOY WILL OVERTAKE THEM,
AND SORROW AND SIGHING WILL FLEE
AWAY. —ISAIAH 51:11 NIV

When one thing goes downhill, it seems everything else follows. Illness prevents you from going about your responsibilities, and work remains undone. Grief dampens your emotions, and you're unable to take pleasure in your activities.

Your faith in God doesn't prevent sadness from coming, but it does give you the strength to handle it. Trusting in his presence, you know you aren't alone, even in the depths of misery. Relying on his power, you receive his comfort and consolation. Believing in his love, you take hold of his promise that he will renew and restore you.

God has compassion on the distressed, for he is the source of joy.

IN THIS WORLD YOU WILL HAVE TROUBLE.
BUT TAKE HEART! I HAVE OVERCOME THE
WORLD. —JOHN 16:33 NIV

God, when things go wrong, strengthen my faith in your presence, and draw me closer to you and the love you have for me. Amen.

God's Promise

# of Protection

EVERY PROMISE OF GOD PROVES TRUE;
HE PROTECTS EVERYONE WHO RUNS TO
HIM FOR HELP. –PROVERBS 30:5-6 MSG

Graceful Words

LET YOUR SPEECH ALWAYS BE WITH GRACE.
—COLOSSIANS 4:6 NASB

Spoken face-to-face, posted on social media, or written in a letter, your words convey more than a message. They express your beliefs and values, and they reflect your standards and principles.

Even when your words aren't overtly about spirituality, they do spiritual work when they come from a heart and mind centered on God's goodness to you and his love for all. Your faith-driven approach to life motivates you to speak well of others, encourage them, and praise their best efforts. Your graceful, grace-filled words not only build them up, but they also build you up.

Whenever you use words, there's an opportunity to bless the lives of others.

THE MOUTH SPEAKS WHAT THE HEART
IS FULL OF. —MATTHEW 12:34 NIV

God, your words convey your love and promises
to me. Help me also to speak graceful words
that will bless those around me. Amen.

Growing in God

GOOD PEOPLE WILL GROW LIKE PALM
TREES. . . . WHEN THEY ARE OLD, THEY WILL
STILL PRODUCE FRUIT. —PSALM 92:12, 14 NCV

Growing in God is an adventure we never out-grow. The more often we reflect on his words and promises, the more our insight deepens, our perception widens, and our understanding increases.

When the Holy Spirit opens our hearts and minds to faith in God, he enables us to grasp essential knowledge, such as God's love and his plan for our salvation. As we think about these truths, we realize that layers of mystery surround them. We ask questions and discover answers, only to find more questions. That's how his Spirit advances his work in us.

No matter how old we are, we're never too old to grow in God.

DRINK DEEP OF GOD'S PURE KINDNESS. THEN
YOU'LL GROW UP MATURE AND WHOLE IN GOD.
—1 PETER 2:2–3 MSG

God, never let me get tired of exploring
Scripture, listening to your voice, hearing your
promises, and growing in faith. Amen.

Doing What's Right

EACH OF YOU SHOULD USE WHATEVER GIFT
YOU HAVE RECEIVED TO SERVE OTHERS, AS
FAITHFUL STEWARDS OF GOD'S GRACE IN ITS
VARIOUS FORMS. —1 PETER 4:10 NIV

Caring for the personal resources God has given us is called stewardship. While we may think of this as a commonsense kind of activity, it takes on a spiritual dimension when we consider that God is our creator as well as the giver of everything we have.

Stewardship begins with the acknowledgment that God has showered us with an astonishing array of gifts and talents. For that reason, we have the responsibility to take care of our resources as we use them and share them with others. We are to do this prayerfully, reflectively, and thoughtfully.

Good stewardship is our response of gratitude to the one whose promises are the source of all.

***

FREELY YOU HAVE RECEIVED; FREELY GIVE.
—MATTHEW 10:8 NIV

***

God, everything I have has come from you. Help me know how best to use what you have so freely given. Amen.

Standing Strong

THE Lord GIVES STRENGTH TO THOSE WHO ARE WEARY. —ISAIAH 40:29 cev

A good night's sleep does wonders for a tired body! But when exhaustion strikes the spirit, it takes more than a nap to restore its energy.

Spiritual weariness can stem from boredom, grief, despondency, or hopelessness. We feel weak and ineffectual, unable to imagine what joy and vitality feel like. This is where God steps in with the promise of his love and care, his understanding and compassion, his assurance that he has good plans for us. Like nothing else, God's power transforms tiredness to liveliness, helplessness to ability.

Be patient with yourself. Lean on him, and let his strength restore, renew, and revitalize your tired spirit.

THE LORD IS MY STRENGTH AND SONG.

—EXODUS 15:2 KJV

God, reenergize my tired spirit. I find my strength in your promises, your understanding, and your continuing direction in my life. Amen.

Calling for Help

GOD, YOUR GOD, IS RIGHT THERE WITH YOU,
FIGHTING WITH YOU AGAINST YOUR ENEMIES,
FIGHTING TO WIN. —DEUTERONOMY 20:4 MSG

Spiritual progress comes with struggle. Though there may be people or circumstances that make our way difficult, far more daunting are inner temptations intent on halting our advancement.

Sin's power to pull us away is strong, but God promises his power to keep us close. When we call for his help, he will answer. If we stumble and fall, he will lift us up and put us on our way again. As forceful as temptation can be, God is more so. In the person of Jesus Christ, he has overcome even death.

When you're struggling, God promises that all you need to do is ask for help.

WE ARE FIGHTING AGAINST FORCES AND
AUTHORITIES AND AGAINST RULERS OF
DARKNESS AND POWERS IN THE SPIRITUAL
WORLD. —EPHESIANS 6:12 CEV

God, remind me to call on you when I struggle. Help me overcome the power of temptation and remain on your path. Amen.

The Light of Life

BY YOUR WORDS I CAN SEE WHERE I'M
GOING; THEY THROW A BEAM OF LIGHT
ON MY DARK PATH. —PSALM 119:105 MSG

Curiosity compels us to dig deeper—perhaps into
a news event, interview, or story. We want to
know more about the subject, so we search for further
information and added details.

As we reflect on Scripture, God's Spirit often stirs our
curiosity. This is when we wonder, *What is God saying
here? What does he mean in this passage?* Our interest
piqued, we might choose to reread the section, con-
sult explanatory notes or a commentary, stop to pray
through our thoughts, or talk to a knowledgeable Christian. God's promise is that the more we study the Bible,
the clearer our spiritual path becomes.

Let your curiosity shed light as you walk in his way.

I WILL STUDY THE WAY THAT IS BLAMELESS.
—PSALM 101:2 NRSV

God, when I'm curious about what I hear or read about you, lead me to your light so that I may grow in understanding. Amen.

The Secret of Success

REMEMBER THE LORD IN ALL YOU DO, AND HE
WILL GIVE YOU SUCCESS. —PROVERBS 3:6 NCV

We wander from or let go of God for many reasons. We release ourselves from him when our will clashes with his. Our enthusiasm for him cools when trouble comes. We give him up to gain the approval of others. But spiritual success depends on our willingness to hang on, despite doubts, questions, obstacles, ridicule, or persecution. He urges us to trust him and believe his promise that he will not let us down.

William Feather, a twentieth-century American writer, once said, "Success seems to be largely a matter of hanging on after others have let go." For genuine success and for lasting success, keep hanging on to God.

BE FAITHFUL UNTIL DEATH, AND I WILL GIVE YOU
THE CROWN OF LIFE. —REVELATION 2:10 NRSV

God, don't let self-will, temptation, or discouragement keep me from hanging on to you, the source of true and lasting success. Amen.

Coming Glory

OUR PRESENT SUFFERINGS ARE NOT WORTH
COMPARING WITH THE GLORY THAT WILL BE
REVEALED IN US. —ROMANS 8:18 NIV

God turns human reasoning inside out. While we prize material possessions, he values spiritual gifts. We push for self-satisfaction, but he prompts us to put others first. In suffering, we find only pain and loss, but through our suffering, God generates spiritual strength and fortitude.

We neither enjoy nor look for suffering, but when God permits it to come into our lives, he turns it around for our good. If there's chaos around us, God works peace within us. If there's anguish or discouragement on the outside, God builds trust, faith, and hope on the inside.

Suffering can be deep—heartbreakingly deep. But God can take it to the heights of glory.

IF YOU SUFFER FOR DOING GOOD AND
YOU ENDURE IT, THIS IS COMMENDABLE
BEFORE GOD. —1 PETER 2:20 NIV

God, in my suffering help me take comfort in
your promises and find peace in the knowledge
of your unending love. Amen.

His Generous Gifts

GOD HAS GIVEN DIFFERENT GIFTS TO EACH
OF US. —1 CORINTHIANS 7:7 cev

Ask ten people what they're good at, and you will get ten different answers. But even if they all were to name the same skill, they would bring their own vision and experience to what they do best.

If you feel that you're not doing your best right now, talk to God. He has given you gifts, skills, and talents unique to you. Allow him to show you how what you do well can bless your life and the lives of others. Invite him to help you reach your potential and discover the joy of being you.

God never skimps when it comes to gifts—his generosity simply won't let him.

USE THE GIFT YOU HAVE.

—1 TIMOTHY 4:14 NCV

God, I'm grateful for your promise to grant me the unique gifts and talents I need to fulfill the plans you have for me. Amen.

Learning from Him

JESUS REPLIED: I AM NOT TEACHING SOMETHING THAT I THOUGHT UP. WHAT I TEACH COMES FROM THE ONE WHO SENT ME.

—JOHN 7:16 CEV

When Jesus wasn't healing the sick, casting out demons, or performing miracles, he was teaching. He taught about love and the power of forgiveness. He taught about the kingdom of God and God's plan for those who trust him. He taught his followers how to live by faith and know their Creator.

And he is still teaching us from the pages of the Bible.

No matter how much you know, there is always so much more to learn from him. Even the Scripture passages you've read many times are full of fresh insights and ageless understanding. As long as you are open to learn, school is in session.

ACCEPT MY TEACHINGS AND LEARN FROM ME,
BECAUSE I AM GENTLE AND HUMBLE IN SPIRIT,
AND YOU WILL FIND REST FOR YOUR LIVES.
—MATTHEW 11:29 NCV

God, open my heart and mind to learn constantly from you, soaking up the powerful lessons in your Word. Amen.

A Way of Escape

GOD CAN BE TRUSTED NOT TO LET YOU
BE TEMPTED TOO MUCH, AND HE WILL
SHOW YOU HOW TO ESCAPE FROM YOUR
TEMPTATIONS. —1 CORINTHIANS 10:13 CEV

Have you ever attended a self-defense class? If you have, you probably learned strategies for staying safe when you're out in public. Your instructor probably taught you to be aware of your surroundings and to be prepared if a threat occurred. And likely you were taught how to slip from the grasp of a predator who intends you harm.

There are strategies designed to keep you safe spiritually as well. Strategies like knowing the Bible, understanding who you are in God, and knowing you can call on him for help will allow you to escape temptation and thwart attempts to destroy your faith.

It's dangerous out there, but God has promised to help.

* * * * * * *

BECAUSE HE HIMSELF SUFFERED WHEN HE WAS TEMPTED, HE IS ABLE TO HELP THOSE WHO ARE BEING TEMPTED. —HEBREWS 2:18 NIV

* * * * * * *

God, thank you for teaching me how to handle myself when temptation strikes and for giving me a way to escape. Amen.

Fully Satisfied

JESUS STOOD AND SHOUTED TO THE CROWDS,
"ANYONE WHO IS THIRSTY MAY COME TO ME!
ANYONE WHO BELIEVES IN ME MAY COME
AND DRINK!" —JOHN 7:37–38 NLT

Traditional wisdom says that after three days without water, the human body will perish. Thirst is much more than an uncomfortable feeling—it's a flashing warning sign that we cannot afford to ignore.

What physical thirst is to the body, spiritual thirst is to the soul. Spiritual thirst is a warning that unless measures are taken, spiritual death is near. God has placed that inner yearning in each of us so that we will run to him—the living water—before we perish spiritually. Once we are fully satisfied, our souls spring to life just as our bodies do when we take a long drink of clean, fresh water. Drink up!

O GOD, YOU ARE MY GOD, I SEEK YOU, MY SOUL
THIRSTS FOR YOU. —PSALM 63:1 NRSV

God, quench my thirst as only you can.
Fill me with your living water that my spirit
within me might spring to life. Amen.

Thoughtful Delights

WHEN MY ANXIOUS THOUGHTS MULTIPLY
WITHIN ME, YOUR CONSOLATIONS DELIGHT
MY SOUL. —PSALM 94:19 NASB

The French philosopher René Descartes made the statement "I think, therefore I am." This may sound inconclusive in its simplicity, but it's true. We identify more quickly with our conscious thoughts than with our physical bodies.

Unfortunately, our amazing minds can also be bastions of confusion, overwhelmed with information, both good and bad. They can provide some awesome flights of fancy, but they can also rob us of our peace.

God has promised to help us discipline our thoughts and use them more profitably. We can keep centered and focused through him. When our thoughts are in sync with his, we become much more than we ever imagined.

* * * * * * *

DON'T COPY THE BEHAVIOR AND CUSTOMS OF THIS WORLD, BUT LET GOD TRANSFORM YOU INTO A NEW PERSON BY CHANGING THE WAY YOU THINK. —ROMANS 12:2 NLT

* * * * * * *

God, I surrender my thoughts to you. Transform my mind as you have promised so that my soul might be delighted in you. Amen.

Someone New

WE ALL, WITH UNVEILED FACE, BEHOLDING
AS IN A MIRROR THE GLORY OF THE
LORD, ARE BEING TRANSFORMED INTO
THE SAME IMAGE FROM GLORY TO GLORY.
—2 CORINTHIANS 3:18 NASB

At one time or another probably most of us have wished we could be someone else, anyone else. Maybe we didn't like our looks or our circumstances, or any number of other things. Have you ever felt that way? Consider this.

God promises that when we give our lives to him, we become someone new. But instead of throwing away the old person we were, he transforms us into a bright, new version of ourselves. Think about what that means. We trade our sins for his holiness, our fears for his fearlessness, and our deficiencies for his all sufficiency. It's like having an all-over makeover.

How great is that?

* * * * * * * *

WE EAGERLY WAIT FOR A SAVIOR, THE LORD JESUS CHRIST: WHO WILL TRANSFORM THE BODY OF OUR HUMBLE STATE INTO CONFORMITY WITH THE BODY OF HIS GLORY. —PHILIPPIANS 3:20–21 NASB

* * * * * * * *

God, I give you my old self, worn out by sin, fear, and inadequacy. Thank you for transforming me into someone you can be proud of. Amen.

God's Promise

of Provision

GOD WILL TAKE CARE OF ALL YOUR NEEDS
WITH THE WONDERFUL BLESSINGS THAT COME
FROM CHRIST JESUS! —PHILIPPIANS 4:19 CEV

Far, Far Away

REMEMBER NOT THE SINS OF MY YOUTH,
NOR MY TRANSGRESSIONS. —PSALM 25:7 KJV

Everyone has broken God's laws and commands. God knew we would transgress when he endowed us with the ability to make choices for ourselves. That's our humanity, but it was important to God for us to choose him.

That's why God devised a plan at the very beginning of all things for the cleansing of those transgressions. He sent his Son, Jesus, to carry the burden of our offenses. Nevertheless. it will always be our choice to make.

When we choose to follow God, God promises that our sins will be washed away, and we will be his beloved children in every way.

I, EVEN I, AM THE ONE WHO WIPES OUT YOUR
TRANSGRESSIONS FOR MY OWN SAKE, AND I WILL
NOT REMEMBER YOUR SINS. —ISAIAH 43:25 NASB

God, I'm so grateful that you gave
me the freedom to choose for myself.
Thank you also for washing away all my
offenses toward you and others. Amen.

Hidden Treasure

SEARCH FOR WISDOM AS YOU WOULD
SEARCH FOR SILVER OR HIDDEN TREASURE.
THEN YOU WILL UNDERSTAND WHAT IT
MEANS TO RESPECT AND TO KNOW THE
LORD GOD. —PROVERBS 2:4–5 CEV

What would you do if someone handed you a treasure map and told you it would lead you to a bounty of hidden treasure? Wouldn't that be great? Someone has. God has given us the Bible. The Bible is a treasure map, capable of leading us to a treasure so vast that we will never want for anything again.

Dig in and you will discover the riches of wisdom and understanding, as well as the precious jewels of love, joy, and peace. There is enough kindness, gentleness, and faithfulness to get you safely through any earthly trial, and that's just the beginning.

Start digging. The treasure is waiting for you to find.

* * * * * * * *

IF SOME ENEMIES BROKE IN AND SEIZED YOUR GOODS, YOU LET THEM GO WITH A SMILE, KNOWING THEY COULDN'T TOUCH YOUR REAL TREASURE. —HEBREWS 10:34 MSG

* * * * * * *

God, your promises are all the treasure I will ever want or need. Guide me as I dig deeply into your Word. Amen.

Stepping-Stones

CONSIDER IT PURE JOY ... WHENEVER YOU FACE TRIALS OF MANY KINDS, BECAUSE YOU KNOW THAT THE TESTING OF YOUR FAITH PRODUCES PERSEVERANCE. —JAMES 1:2–3 NIV

Trials and tribulations are no fun. If they disappeared completely, no one would miss them. Nevertheless, they do serve a purpose in God's economy. Trials are like stepping-stones. They create a path for us as we grow in our faith and our quest to become the people God has created us to be.

Trials fall into common categories, but they often are also specific and personal for each of us. God doesn't send tribulations our way, but he does use them to teach and strengthen us, wasting nothing. God promises that whatever we might encounter in this life, he will use it for our eternal good.

WE CONTINUE TO SHOUT OUR PRAISE EVEN WHEN
WE'RE HEMMED IN WITH TROUBLES, BECAUSE WE
KNOW HOW TROUBLES CAN DEVELOP PASSIONATE
PATIENCE IN US, AND HOW THAT PATIENCE IN
TURN FORGES THE TEMPERED STEEL OF VIRTUE.
—ROMANS 5:3-4 MSG

God, thank you for taking all the trials in my
life and using them to help me become the
person you created me to be. Amen.

Trusting Jesus

EVERY CHILD OF GOD DEFEATS THIS EVIL
WORLD, AND WE ACHIEVE THIS VICTORY
THROUGH OUR FAITH. —1 JOHN 5:4 NLT

At the end of a reality courtroom television show, the losing plaintiff often says, "Don't ever trust anyone." Sounds like good advice, but it's quite unrealistic. None of us lives in a vacuum.

We have to place a certain amount of trust in others—our children's teachers, our local pharmacist, and the police, to name just a few.

The truth is that all human beings are going to let us down, some sooner than others. No one is completely trustworthy—except God. He alone has the power, the resources, the time, and the will to ensure that he will never disappoint us. He alone is truly worthy of our trust.

GOD BLESSES EVERYONE WHO TRUSTS HIM.
—PROVERBS 16:20 CEV

God, help me to trust others when I must. I trust you always, knowing that you will never let me down. Amen.

Every True Word

I HAVE ALWAYS BEEN MINDFUL OF YOUR
UNFAILING LOVE AND HAVE LIVED IN RELIANCE
ON YOUR FAITHFULNESS. —PSALM 26:3 NIV

It's important for every believer to know the truth preserved in the pages of the Bible—God's Holy Word—because the truth written there is power. Once we know the truth, we are well armed, no longer vulnerable to those who would try to manipulate, discourage, or confuse us.

When we know the truth about us, that we are God's own children, no one can take away our confidence or destroy our sense of worth. When we know the truth about God's promises, no one can cheat us out of all God has given us.

Truth frees us from the back talk of our spiritual enemies and continually affirms God's love for us.

YOU WILL KNOW THE TRUTH, AND THE TRUTH
WILL MAKE YOU FREE. —JOHN 8:32 NCV

God, thank you for truth. It sets
me free to become the person you
created me to be. Amen.

Know and Understand

TO HAVE UNDERSTANDING, YOU MUST KNOW
THE HOLY GOD. —PROVERBS 9:10 cev

Have you heard the phrase "to know him is to love him"? Of course it is talking about human relationships, but we could actually say those words about our heavenly Father.

The more we know him, the more we understand what great lengths he went to in order to redeem us. The more we know him, the more we understand the vast benefits he brings to our lives.

The more we know him, the more we are aware of his great promises, the more we realize his magnificent love for us, and the more we feel compelled to love him in return.

THIS ENDLESS KNOWING AND UNDERSTANDING—
ALL THIS CAME THROUGH JESUS, THE MESSIAH.
—JOHN 1:17 MSG

God, to know you is to love you. Thank you for all the wonderful benefits you have brought to my life. Amen.

Standing as One

MAY . . . GOD DEVELOP MATURITY IN YOU
SO THAT YOU GET ALONG WITH EACH
OTHER AS WELL AS JESUS GETS ALONG
WITH US ALL. —ROMANS 15:5–6 msg

D on't make me come in there," Dad calls out to siblings arguing in the next room. Disagreeing is a fact of family life—really, a fact of life itself. Since God created each of us as unique individuals and endowed us with free will, we won't always agree. But who says that's not a good thing?

God doesn't expect us to agree about everything. Instead he asks us to love and respect each other. The exchange of varying views and opinions can spawn great ideas and creativity. That's how most of our world's greatest accomplishments came about.

We have our differences, but when we work together? Wow! That's when we truly shine.

* * * * * * * *

MAY [THE DISCIPLES AND ALL WHO BELIEVE IN ME] EXPERIENCE SUCH PERFECT UNITY THAT THE WORLD WILL KNOW THAT YOU SENT ME. —JOHN 17:23 NLT

* * * * * * * *

God, thanks for the excitement we experience when we work together and appreciate our differences. Amen.

Others First

DO NOT BE INTERESTED ONLY IN YOUR OWN LIFE, BUT BE INTERESTED IN THE LIVES OF OTHERS. —PHILIPPIANS 2:4 NCV

Spend a little time with a small child and you will see unfettered selfishness. We come into this world believing that we are the center of the universe. But, of course, that universe is pretty small.

As we mature, we learn to accept that we share the spotlight with many others who matter just as much as we do. The Bible tells us that putting others before ourselves is a sign of spiritual maturity. We learn that Jesus, God's only Son, laid down his limitless rights and privileges for our sake.

Through his example, we learn that self is not diminished when we put others first. Rather, self is enhanced in the right way when we put others first.

IF ANY OF YOU WANTS TO BE MY FOLLOWER,
YOU MUST GIVE UP YOUR OWN WAY,
TAKE UP YOUR CROSS, AND FOLLOW ME.
—MARK 8:34 NLT

God, help me to truly see those around me
and truly care about their needs more than
I care about my own. Amen.

Celebrating the Victory

THANKS BE TO GOD, WHO GIVES US THE VICTORY THROUGH OUR LORD JESUS CHRIST. —1 CORINTHIANS 15:57 NRSV

Winning is a good feeling. When a runner crosses that finish line, he feels an overwhelming sense of euphoria. He forgets all his stumbles, missteps, and moments of doubt.

We are all in a race called life. We sprint through our days, determined to overcome the obstacles, ignoring our aching limbs and labored breathing. We want to know that our lives mean something, that we haven't lived in vain.

God promises us victory in the race of life—a straight-up win. He also promises to be with us along the way, and he offers encouragement and living water. When we cross that finish line, he'll be there cheering us on.

*   *   *   *   *   *   *

HOLDING FAST THE WORD OF LIFE, SO THAT I MAY REJOICE IN THE DAY OF CHRIST THAT I HAVE NOT RUN IN VAIN OR LABORED IN VAIN.
—PHILIPPIANS 2:16 NKJV

*   *   *   *   *   *   *

God, thank you for being my coach as I run the race of life. With your help and encouragement, I am guaranteed the victory. Amen.

Much Wealth

HONOR THE LORD WITH YOUR WEALTH AND
WITH THE BEST PART OF EVERYTHING YOU
PRODUCE. —PROVERBS 3:9 NLT

Most of us have dreamed about what it would be like to have all the money we could want or need. No more worries about bills. We could provide our families with all the finer things. Plenty of troubling circumstances would disappear.

But money can't solve every problem. Ask any lottery winner. Money can't insulate us from fear, heartache, tragedy, disappointment, or embarrassment. Money can't buy love, happiness, or peace with God. In fact, some wealthy individuals say the only gratifying advantage to having money is using it to help others.

The better way? To have a wealthy heavenly Father who has promised to meet all our needs.

WE ARE POOR, BUT WE GIVE SPIRITUAL RICHES
TO OTHERS. WE OWN NOTHING, AND YET WE
HAVE EVERYTHING. —2 CORINTHIANS 6:10 NLT

God, thank you for meeting all my needs.
I would much rather put my trust in you
than in all that riches have to offer. Amen.

Strength for Weakness

THE Lord IS MY STRENGTH AND MY SHIELD;
IN HIM MY HEART TRUSTS, SO I AM HELPED,
AND MY HEART EXULTS. —PSALM 28:7 NRSV

As a child, did you ever look up at your earthly father and imagine him to be the strongest, most powerful man on earth? Many children see their fathers that way. Only as we grow older do we realize that earthly bodies can't sustain the physical strength of earlier years.

Our heavenly Father's strength will never fail. He will always be there to defend us, rescue us, and carry us when we have no strength of our own. God's unlimited resources, complete understanding, and almighty purpose comprise his strength. He cannot be defeated.

Our earthly fathers will one day fail us simply because they are human, but our heavenly Father never will.

MY FLESH AND MY HEART MAY FAIL, BUT
GOD IS THE STRENGTH OF MY HEART AND
MY PORTION FOREVER. —PSALM 73:26 NRSV

God, I place my trust in you, knowing you will always be there, eternally strong, mighty, and sufficient to meet my every need. Amen.

God Is Great

TAKE A GOOD LOOK AT GOD'S WONDERS—
THEY'LL TAKE YOUR BREATH AWAY.
—PSALM 66:5 MSG

Encyclopedias used to proclaim there were seven "wonders of the world." That list, which included the Great Wall of China as well as the Great Pyramid of Giza, has been revised and lengthened countless times. Newer lists, which include still more man-made "wonders" from the Golden Gate Bridge to the Panama Canal, also fall short.

What about the starry sky, a field of wildflowers, or the majesty of an ocean? What would our heavenly Father say is the greatest?

Given his redemptive actions concerning us, God might feel that we are the greatest of his wonders. He created us in his own image, and we are uniquely his. How much more wonderful could anything else be?

[GOD] CREATED THE SKIES AND STRETCHED THEM OUT. HE SPREAD OUT THE EARTH AND EVERYTHING ON IT. HE GIVES LIFE TO ALL PEOPLE ON EARTH, TO EVERYONE WHO WALKS ON THE EARTH. —ISAIAH 42:5 NCV

God, thank you for your great creative hand that gave me life. I am honored to be one of your great wonders. Amen.

Wholeness in God

MAY YOUR SPIRIT AND SOUL AND BODY
BE KEPT SOUND AND BLAMELESS AT THE
COMING OF OUR LORD JESUS CHRIST.
—1 THESSALONIANS 5:23 NRSV

I n *The Wizard of Oz*, the Tin Man, the Scarecrow, and the Cowardly Lion are on a quest to find their missing parts. The Tin Man wants a heart, the Scarecrow wants a brain, and the Lion wants some courage. Though they looked just fine, they knew they weren't whole without them.

Their lack illustrates what we human beings all know. We're more than just bodies; we're complex creations. When something is missing, we feel it.

We were created with three parts: a spirit, a soul, and a body. God is the True Wizard. He is faithful to care for all parts of his creation.

HIS NAMES WILL BE: AMAZING COUNSELOR, STRONG GOD, ETERNAL FATHER, PRINCE OF WHOLENESS. HIS RULING AUTHORITY WILL GROW, AND THERE'LL BE NO LIMITS TO THE WHOLENESS HE BRINGS.
—ISAIAH 9:6–7 MSG

God, thank you for creating me in your image. Thank you for your promise to make me whole in every way. Amen.

He Who Is Wise

[GOD] GIVES WISDOM TO THE WISE AND
KNOWLEDGE TO THOSE WHO HAVE
UNDERSTANDING. —DANIEL 2:21 NRSV

There are a lot of smart people in this world—people who can rattle off facts and figures, explain complex concepts, and skillfully solve puzzles. Many fewer people, however, know how to live their lives successfully.

Intelligence is something we're born with. Wisdom, however, is something that comes from learning life's lessons. It's defined as insight, good sense, or sound judgment.

You may or may not qualify for Mensa membership, but God has promised that wisdom is far more valuable and is yours for the asking. Sure, it will probably come with a lesson attached, but if you're a good student, you'll end up way ahead.

IF ANY OF YOU LACKS WISDOM, LET HIM ASK
OF GOD, WHO GIVES TO ALL LIBERALLY AND
WITHOUT REPROACH, AND IT WILL BE GIVEN
TO HIM. —JAMES 1:5 NKJV

God, thank you for teaching me the life
lessons that will make me wise and able to
live my life successfully. Amen.

Unto the Lord

THE LORD YOUR GOD WILL BLESS YOU IN
ALL YOUR HARVEST AND IN ALL THE WORK
OF YOUR HANDS, AND YOUR JOY WILL BE
COMPLETE. –DEUTERONOMY 16:15 NIV

Throughout the Bible, we find references to "the work of God's hands." These include things like establishing the expanses of the heavens, the moon and the stars, the dry land, the depths of the earth, the peaks of the mountains, the lightning, and the sunlight. God did all that in addition to instituting truth and justice and creating humankind.

God rested on the seventh day, but until then he was quite busy getting things done. It would seem that he wants us to do the same. Our work encompasses working at jobs, raising families, and helping others.

When we do our work, God promises to bless and establish what we do.

LET THE BEAUTY OF THE Lord OUR GOD BE UPON US, AND ESTABLISH THE WORK OF OUR HANDS FOR US. —PSALM 90:17 NKJV

God, thank you for blessing the work of my hands. And thank you for giving me rest when my work is done. Amen.

Don't Worry

DON'T FRET OR WORRY. INSTEAD OF WORRYING,
PRAY. LET PETITIONS AND PRAISES SHAPE YOUR
WORRIES INTO PRAYERS, LETTING GOD KNOW
YOUR CONCERNS. . . . IT'S WONDERFUL WHAT
HAPPENS WHEN CHRIST DISPLACES WORRY AT
THE CENTER OF YOUR LIFE. —PHILIPPIANS 4:6–7 MSG

Wouldn't most of us like to live in a world where we would never worry again? All our needs would be met and all our loved ones safe. Our physical bodies would behave just as they were created to behave, regardless of their years of use.

There is such a place, of course. It's called heaven. For now, however, we live in a world filled with sin and imperfection. And we have no guarantees.

The good news is that we don't walk through this life alone. God promises he will see us through whatever life brings. He will hold tightly to our hands as we give our worries to him in prayer.

＊ ＊ ＊ ＊ ＊ ＊ ＊ ＊

I AM LEAVING YOU WITH A GIFT—PEACE OF MIND AND HEART. AND THE PEACE I GIVE IS A GIFT THE WORLD CANNOT GIVE. SO DON'T BE TROUBLED OR AFRAID. —JOHN 14:27 NLT

＊ ＊ ＊ ＊ ＊ ＊ ＊ ＊

God, thank you for walking through this life with me and for seeing that whatever I have to face, I will not face it alone. Amen.

Worship Him

THANK HIM. WORSHIP HIM. FOR GOD IS
SHEER BEAUTY, ALL-GENEROUS IN LOVE,
LOYAL ALWAYS AND EVER. —PSALM 100:4–5 MSG

What's the deal with God? Why does he want to be worshiped? Does it seem that he is on an ego trip? Some of us argued this line of reasoning with our parents when we were teenagers. But as we matured, we began to see things differently.

When God demands respect and reverence—what the Bible calls *fear*—from us, it is for our sake, not his. He is only able to help us when we are convinced that he is willing and able to do so.

God has no need to be reminded of who he is. We are the ones with faulty memory. Worship keeps us focused on his greatness to meet our needs.

SHE CAME AND WORSHIPED HIM, SAYING,
"LORD, HELP ME!" —MATTHEW 15:25 NKJV

God, you are beyond worthy of my love and worship. Thank you for reminding me that you are able to see me through any situation. Amen.

God's Promise

of Eternal Life

THIS IS THE PROMISE WHICH HE HIMSELF
MADE TO US: ETERNAL LIFE. —1 JOHN 2:25 NASB

You May Also Like . . .

365 Moments of Peace for a Woman's Heart offers inspiring psalms and meditations to calm and comfort you throughout your day. In these pages you will rest in the loving presence of your God, find a haven from the pressures of daily life, and learn that God's perfect peace can be yours in the midst of any circumstance.

365 Moments of Peace for a Woman's Heart

You're invited into God's presence, where the gift of peace awaits. In the pages of this book you will come to know God more intimately and understand His constant love for you. He is waiting to fill you with joy and assure you that He is with you every step of your journey. Live in the light of His love.

Moments of Peace in the Presence of God